Wife OF THE CHEF

Wife

OF THE CHEF

COURTNEY FEBBRORIELLO

CLARKSON POTTER/
PUBLISHERS
New York

A portion was originally published in
The Washington Post.

Published by Clarkson Potter/Publishers,
New York, New York. Member of the
Crown Publishing Group, a division of
Random House, Inc. New York, Toronto,
London, Sydney, Auckland
www.randomhouse.com

CLARKSON N. POTTER is a trademark and
POTTER and colophon are registered trademarks
of Random House, Inc.

Printed in U.S.A.

Design by Marysarah Quinn

Library of Congress
Cataloging-in-Publication Data

Febbroriello, Courtney.
Wife of the chef / Courtney Febbroriello.
p. cm.
1. Febbroriello, Courtney. 2. Wives—United
States—Connecticut—Biography.
3. Prosperi, Christopher.
4. Cooks—United States—Connecticut—
Biography. 5. Metro Bis. I. Title.
TX910.3 .F43 2003
641.5'092—dc21   2002005984

ISBN 0-609-61106-2

10 9 8 7 6 5 4 3 2 1

FIRST EDITION

CONTENTS

PROLOGUE

THE RESTAURANT

Metro Bis is a sixty-four-seat bistro in Simsbury, Connecticut, twenty miles west of Hartford. I've owned the place with my chef husband for the last three years. Metro Bis is small, loud, and classically decorated with a wooden floor, a long banquette that runs down the right-hand side of the room, and French lace curtains on the windows to the left. There is a service bar in the entryway with a large antique window hanging from the ceiling that acts as a wineglass holder. The twenty linen-covered tables are divided into three rows that run the length of the room. The tables along the windows have wooden school chairs. The tables in the middle and on the banquette have chairs with rounded dark green arms.

At the end of the dining room, an enormous hutch partially blocks the view of the kitchen, eliminating the need for doors. All the diners can see is the dessert station, straight back on the right of the hutch, and the upper bodies of the chefs on the left of the hutch. This large piece of furniture hides the plating line that separates the pickup and dishwashing area from the stove, grill, Fry-O-Lator, salad station, and chefs on the other side.

My husband and I are the second owners of Metro Bis, having purchased the restaurant on August 12, 1998. The name came from the previous owners, who had operated another place, called Metro Kitchen, in a nearby town. They opened Metro Bis (Bis means "again" or "encore" in French) and closed Metro Kitchen five years before we purchased the restaurant. They used the Paris Metro as a theme because one of the ex-owners' family had helped to modernize and refurbish the subway system. We still have a set of old wooden train doors by the computer, and the four lanterns along the ceiling are from a Metro station.

For this reason, we kept the name even when we changed the cuisine from upscale French to American bistro. The menu features bistro fare with an Asian influence and a couple of delicate upscale items. There's steak, salmon, pasta, foie gras, spring rolls, caviar, and leg of lamb at dinner. Lunch includes some of the same with a mix of sandwiches and salads. Each month Metro Bis creates a five-course wine dinner with dishes not usually found on the menu. We are open six days a week, serving lunch and dinner every day but Sunday.

Most of the staff at Metro Bis have been working with us for over a year. Our longest and most trusted employee is Jerry, the general manager. Customers find him strikingly attractive, cordial, and firmly in command of the dining room. The waitstaff think Jerry is rigid, demanding, and private. I think he's hysterical. Jerry has an unbelievable sense of humor. He's also very set in his ways. There is no gray (other than in his hair) in Jerry's life; there is only black and white, right and wrong. He has an endearing sensitive side that only comes out around children. He's like an older brother to me and a great friend. Jerry would catch a burning tree that was about to fall on me if I couldn't save myself, but he would never admit that he had done it. He's committed to the restaurant business and is always challenging himself to learn more. His next goal is to pass the master sommelier exam. My husband, Jerry, and I met while working in another Connecticut restaurant, where we also met Al, our first sous-chef. Al recently moved on in his career and was replaced by Norman.

My chef husband and I also operate a tiny takeout store in the same shopping complex where the restaurant is located. Metro Express features wraps, soups, salads, and microwavable entrées. There's also a kids' menu, a catering menu, and a picnic-basket menu for events, like the outdoor concert series that takes place behind the building each summer. We also do a complete meal to go for each of the major holidays. Valentine's Day, Easter, Thanksgiving, Christmas, and New Year's are busy holidays for Metro Express. In between these events, the staff is busy with the two-thousand-person mailing list and the bottling of our salad dressing. We produce fifteen gallons a week of Prosperi balsamic, tomato ginger, and Caesar dressings. We run between the office, storage room, Metro Express, and Metro Bis all day long.

THE CHEF

My husband, Christopher Prosperi, and I have been married for three years but have known each other for eight. We met at a restaurant in Connecticut where he was a chef and I was an ice cream scooper. Chris's whole family is in the restaurant business, including his European-born parents. He grew up in Forest Hills, New York, and moved to Connecticut while in high school. Chris is good-humored and he's messy. Most of his friends call him scatterbrained and think of him as the artistic type. I married him because he's so even-tempered, we have common goals, and we rarely disagree. He's as committed as you would expect anyone who worked with you fourteen hours a day to be, and he's exceptionally creative. If that burning tree I mentioned earlier were about to fall on me, Chris wouldn't notice until someone called him from the hospital. Then he would rush to my side with flowers, pillows, and food. Chris would care for me around the clock until he needed to check on the restaurant. Then he would go back to work. Chris is committed to his profession and he loves food, but he doesn't take it too seriously.

Frequently I am asked how Chris and I can work together all day and still have a relationship. I hardly ever see Chris during the day. The most I ever see him is while he is sleeping at night. My typical day consists of shuttling from the restaurant to the office to our takeout store and back again, with a trip to the post office, the bank, and storage in between. Chris travels a bit as well, but we're hardly ever in the same place at the same time. Most of his day is spent in the kitchen, and most of mine is spent in the office. As we run past each other, conversation is limited to the tasks at hand:

"I just booked us for Sunday the twenty-fifth for dinner."

"How many orders of bread do you have going out of Express this weekend?"

"Have you had time to make udon noodles yet?"

"Did you see that e-mail?"

"What do you think we should do about the line cook?"

"I made you a dentist appointment for next Tuesday."

At the end of the day when we are back at home, all we talk about is work. We plan how we might take over the world, what connections need to be made, what gossip has been heard, what to do about troubled employees, and what we should spend money on.

But we do have some serious gaps in communication, as the staff can attest to. Chris and I drive everyone insane. Half the time they don't know when we are coming and going. Chris will tell the sous-chef that there is a charity event we are attending on Wednesday. The sous-chef will adjust the schedule, but then I'll come upstairs and tell him the event is on Thursday. Sometimes we only remember at the last possible second that there is another place we need to be.

Chris also has an interesting theory of information transmitting. We might go to a friend's house, where I find out that her mother died suddenly in a car accident. I'm in shock, I feel bad, and I didn't bring the obligatory card or flowers. The friend looks at me disbelievingly and says, "I talked to Chris about it three days ago. Didn't he tell you?"

In the car on the way home I might say, "Why didn't you tell me that Sarah's mother died last week?"

"You didn't ask."

Chris is also infamous for transferring a call from my father to the office and saying, "This is your dad. He called you earlier today and wanted you to call him back."

It's almost as if he can remember only ten pieces of information at a time. When new data enters his brain, an old piece is left behind regardless of its importance.

I'm not sure how we work together, but we do. It's probably a combination of not seeing each other and our inability to communicate. We're on the same ship, trying to reach the same destination, and it would be foolish to argue about where we are headed. There isn't enough time for petty disagreements, for grudges, for blame. We work well together because there is little competition between us. Each of us knows our strengths and weaknesses. What one lacks, the other makes up for. I can cook only two things from scratch without a recipe: meat loaf, which I don't eat, and macaroni and cheese, which I don't have to make because we serve it at Express. Chris isn't capable of organizing the business and paying the bills. He's great at solving conflicts. He has good networking skills. I do the marketing. I write *Metro Mail*, the restaurant's newsletter. I plot. I plan. I come up with new ways to make money. If the two of us can't do a job, we find someone else who can. Somehow it all works out in the end.

THE WIFE

I grew up in a tiny town in Connecticut as the daughter of a divorce lawyer and a housewife. I have a younger brother and sister, Jared and Devin. My mother had been a middle-school English teacher who insisted on sending me to private school when she realized that I couldn't spell or memorize my multiplication tables. I got my first restaurant job during my senior year of high school after being bored to death answering the phones in my father's office. I just couldn't sit still that long. Throughout my college career, I kept on working in restaurants for extra spending money, and I loved it. Higher education seemed like a waste of time, despite my desire to secure an English degree and certification to teach secondary school, so I finished in three years.

The best part about college was meeting my roommate, Kate. She has a lot of the same thoughts as I do, but she is much more quiet about them, which keeps her out of trouble. Kate understands me better than anyone else. We like to go on adventures together, and she is one of the few people

I travel well with. Kate would see that burning tree about to fall and point it out to me way before I was in any danger. Then we would talk about what we should do with the tree. Is it more important to put the fire out, or prevent it from falling over? I would decide it was best to leave it alone after Kate suggested as much, but I'd probably find her stuck underneath it a couple minutes later, unable to follow her own advice. Kate has known me for as long as Chris has, and she even lived with us in our three-room apartment for four months when she moved to the East Coast from California. She loves to eat in restaurants, but she'd never work in one.

While I was completing my degree, I was working full-time as a waitress and was living with Chris. Still, I felt I should have a "legitimate" career because my parents had paid so much for private education, so I began my master's degree in marriage and family therapy. (Very handy, it turns out, in the restaurant business.) I finished all of my coursework and was about to begin my yearlong internship when I married my chef and opened a restaurant. There's nothing too extraordinary about this except that I'm a vegetarian, I don't drink, and I look like I'm twelve (on a good day).

A RESTAURANT is often compared to a theater. The audience/diners never see behind the curtain. They don't know that our line cook was smoking out back and a waiter was late because he had a fight with his wife. More important, they don't know me, but they think they do. I want to tell people that the restaurant business isn't a glorious romantic experience. It's a lot of really hard work filled with curveballs they would never expect. I'm tired of people in the dining room telling me that they want to run a small inn with six rooms and serve breakfast when they retire. I'm tired of high-school students thinking that they will go to culinary school and become famous TV chefs a year after graduation. Mostly I'm tired of people sighing as they look at me and say, "The restaurant business is so hard. The hours are so long. You must really love what you do."

I do love what I do, but not for the reasons they think I should. I don't love waiting on people. It isn't like hosting a dinner party every night. I love what I do because it is a challenge. Being on the floor is like wearing a mask. People think that I am the gracious hostess of the year, but I'm not. I'm just a person like everyone else, working my ass off to make a living.

I'm pretty anal retentive. I notice everything. Nothing, nothing, nothing is ever good enough for me. I see every chip in the paint, every grain of sand in the entryway, and every stray hair in the bathroom. Chris can't find the knife that he's holding in his hand, but I notice that the bread baskets need to be cleaned, and the shelf where he stores too many dry products is separating from the wall. Chris won't notice it until it hits the floor during a slow afternoon. This bothersome drive for perfection leaves me frustrated and unfulfilled. Everything must be bigger, better, cleaner, faster.

I don't have time to wonder why or how I was pulled into this business. The romance has long disappeared, my body aches, and all I can think about is getting everything ready in time for lunch. Perhaps it is the stress, the drive, the energy involved in pulling off service so smoothly that makes it so no one can tell that we cleaned the lettuce as we plated it or that we tripped over the refrigeration man's toolbox as he fixed the ailing walk-in during an emergency call. Or it could be the challenge of serving a public who raves over your scallop dish but complains that some of the baby *greens* are red. Maybe it's the unpredictability of it all: twenty-three people for lunch today and ninety-six tomorrow; the case of wine dropped on the way to storage; the corn that never made it to the kitchen in time for dinner. Why is such instability, organized chaos, and insanity craved by so many people in this business and, more particularly, why me?

At no other time in my life have I felt more challenged, confident, overwhelmed, and consequently more alive than I do working in this business. Every day I am forced to learn something new about food, service, marketing, finances, and, most important, myself. I understand my limitations and find ways to work with others to accomplish my goals. I cherish my strengths and use them every moment of my day because I am more creative, resourceful, responsible, and flexible than I could ever be while sitting behind a desk.

And I love it. This constant education and stimulation gives me the energy to keep on going when one of the floor staff doesn't show up on a holiday or someone in the kitchen knocks over a five-gallon bucket of chicken stock.

When I drag myself back to bed at the end of the day, I have time to think about all of the things that didn't get done and everything that I wish I had time for. There is so much that I want to learn, to experience, to eat. How can a sixteen-hour-day go by so quickly? Wasn't I supposed to discuss my food costing with the accountant, make seasonal menu changes, and call the newspaper to put in another help-wanted add? It would be nice to take a culinary tour of the world, publish a cookbook, and make guest appearances on the Food Network, but I would settle for a more organized restaurant that allowed me the time to scrutinize daily sales, promote the business while outside the building, and plan my next expansion project.

But these things take time that I don't have yet. For now I joyfully struggle knowing that I am exactly where I belong: in a demanding yet fulfilling profession that strives to make something as simple as sustaining life into an extraordinary experience.

HER LOVER

What kind of person do you think I am?

I'm only kidding. It's not that kind of book.

INTRODUCTION

*T*he first time I encountered Christopher Prosperi, I was working in an ice cream shop in New Milford, Connecticut, during my holiday break in college. Chris was working across the street as a chef in an upscale bistro owned by the same guy who owned the ice cream shop. Because December and January are slow months in the ice cream business, the restaurant would send someone over with prep work from the kitchen.

I was often sent the dreaded case of basil or spinach to pick—dishwashers were too skilled and their time too valuable for that task. If you've ever plucked the leaves off an entire case of basil, then you know that the aroma is overwhelming, that it'll make your hands reek for at least three days, and that it doesn't really go with ice cream. One day I asked for something different. Something more challenging. Maybe I would get to use a peeler or a knife.

Instead I received black olives. These were not the black olives that I was used to, however. They didn't have those entertaining holes used by children as a place to stick their fingers. They didn't even come in a can. No, these were

Kalamata olives and they arrived in a five-gallon bucket. Pits included. It would be my job to remove the pits.

Chris actually demonstrated the squeezing procedure necessary for pitting. Then he carefully separated the pit from the flesh in each hand and looked at me very intently.

"This is the pit," he said slowly. "And this is the part that we keep."

He held up each piece so that there would be no confusion. I fought back the urge to say, "Bite me," and got to work. He wandered back across the street to the kitchen while I spent the day pitting the olives. And I do mean the whole day. It took me a full five hours to pit those five gallons of olives. I'll never forget that stubborn flesh forced between my thumb and index finger, the squeezing and squishing that eventually yielded the unwanted pit.

When I had finished my task, I called the restaurant to tell them I was done. One of the staff came to retrieve my olives. I handed her a bucket of all the pits I had squeezed from the olives—I had carefully saved each one—and asked her to make sure that they reached Chris before the flesh. She came back almost immediately to say that when he received them, he looked at her, wondered for a minute if I had really kept the wrong part, looked back at the pits, realized that I was messing with him, called me a smart-ass, and threw them away. I knew I was in love. Well, maybe not quite yet.

1
LUNCH

ASSEMBLING
THE TROOPS

$\mathcal{T}$oday I am only half awake when I feel Chris kiss my cheek. "I love you," he whispers. Then he takes five steps into the living room, picks up the phone, and speaks in his usual megaphone voice. "HELLO, IS CHAD THERE? CHAD, I FORGOT TO ORDER FISH LAST NIGHT. IS IT TOO LATE? GOOD. I NEED A MEDIUM SALMON AND A BOX OF 21 / 25s. AND SEND ME FIFTEEN POUNDS OF WHATEVER YOU HAVE THAT'S GOOD. THANKS, MAN. I'LL TALK TO YOU LATER TODAY." Then he clomps down the stairs in his navy blue rubber clogs and slams the front door. Fully awake, I open my eyes just enough to read the red digital clock. Seven thirty-one. The time glows even after I squeeze my eyes shut and roll over to the cool side of the pillow. As I quickly drift back to sleep, I know that it won't be for long. I vaguely remember a work-related nightmare that I have been fighting all night. Something about a line of people at the door and no chairs anywhere in the restaurant to seat them. At 7:54 I roll back toward the clock. I'm pretty sure that I went to bed at two, and I'm positive that I need to go to the bathroom. I slowly push my legs off the side of the warm bed, sit up, and eventually end up on the couch with a glass of orange juice, flipping between Headline News, the Travel Channel, the Weather Channel, and, of course, the Food Network. When I am finally awake enough to function, I jump in the shower, pull an outfit off of the floor, and head for the car.

As I walk across the front yard, I am accosted by my next-door neighbor. She has a concern about the maintenance of the building we share. I don't spend much time at home, and I can't be bothered with shoveling, raking, mowing, and garbage removal. (The landlord finally gave us our own garbage pail so that we would be responsible for taking it to the street rather than allowing it to overflow in the backyard.) As my neighbor prattles on about one such issue (I'm not really listening), I attempt, politely, to get into my car. Then she stops midsentence and asks, "Don't you own your own business? With your boyfriend?"

"My husband."

"Then you must understand what I'm talking about. I own my own hairdressing business."

I manage a sympathetic smile until she says, "Oh, but I'm sure it's easier for you because you own it with your husband."

I get in my car and drive away.

The ride to Metro Bis is just under twenty minutes. I constantly flip between radio stations, trying to find music. Chris likes to listen to the news in his car, but his stereo has been broken for six months. I don't know why I bother to change the channels; I'm not really listening, anyway. I'm thinking about the two caterings that are going out of Metro Express, the tomato ginger salad dressing that needs to be repacked because it separated, the twenty-seven dinner reservations, and the new guy who needs to fill out paperwork today. When I pull into the parking lot, I have a good idea of what I'm going to do first. By the time I get from the bar to the office, my plans have evaporated.

I always start the workday by entering the front door of the restaurant. This is the first place customers see when entering; it's where they get their first impression. As I fly through the door, I straighten the menus and replenish the business cards on the display table to the left. I pull the paperwork from yesterday's sales. I check the reservations for tonight. We're up to thirty-four people and lunch hasn't even started. I answer the phone and take a reservation for Saturday. Jerry, our manager, greets me, smiling with a hearty and sarcastic "Good morning, Sunshine!" He asks when I'm going to put out the next *Metro Mail* and tells me that he has been bugging Chris all morning to finish the Mondavi wine dinner menu. As usual, Chris has been attached to the phone since nine A.M. I've been thinking about implanting a phone in his head. Before I can answer Jerry, the phone rings again. It's the produce company trying to get an order from Chris. I already know where he is, though I haven't seen him yet. I can hear him "chatting" at the top of his lungs not more than sixty feet from me, on the other phone in the back of the dining room. As I'm walking toward the kitchen, I tell Jerry that I will have a *Metro Mail* done by dinner tonight. I stop by table eight and glance at Chris. He's always smiling, so I can't tell if he's happy to see me or just having a good conversation. I quickly realize he's just gossiping, which is part of his morning routine. There is a whole network of underground restaurant information transmitted daily by salesmen with the dirt on job openings and sales figures. I tell Chris that the produce company is on line two. While he switches lines, I poke through the paperwork on table eight. All of our staff jokingly call the two-top closest to the kitchen Chris's desk. I kicked him out of the restaurant's real office. After the first three months of sharing it with him, he left a dirty crème brûlée dish underneath a stack of papers on the desk. I cleaned the ants, the dish, his papers, and Chris out of the office the next day. He eventually settled on table eight. It was originally a table for four until Jerry decided he couldn't stand the mess either and took half of the "desk" away. Today there are a couple of phone messages for me and a fax for an upcoming March of Dimes event. I add them to the receipts from yesterday, roll my eyes at Chris, and head for the kitchen. He waves as I walk away, looking as though he'll be on the phone for at least another twenty minutes.

Everyone in the kitchen looks pretty busy, but it's very quiet. The caffeine won't really kick in until the middle of lunch. The dishwasher already has a pile of dishes in the pot sink from the early-morning prep work that Chris must have done before he got on the phone. Instead of doing the dishes, he's busy dumping out the Fry-O-Lator oil into a five-gallon bucket. We do it in the morning when the oil is cool. Chris once had a line cook who emptied the hot oil into a plastic bucket at the end of the night. As the pail melted, an ocean of oil was released over the kitchen, floating rafts of French fries and extra-crispy calamari. It was funny to everyone except the line cook, who spent the next two hours cleaning it up. Today the dishwasher still needs to degrease the Fry-O-Lator bay, refill it with fresh oil, and put the old oil in the grease Dumpster. (Cosmetic companies make lipstick and other products that I would never use from the recycled oil.) The lunch chef is setting up his station. Chris is still on the phone. I grab the invoices off the back bulletin board and head out the door.

Metro Bis is located in an old shopping center. We rent four spaces: the restaurant, office, storage, and Metro Express, the takeout store. In order to get to the office, I walk out the kitchen door, down a flight of stairs, past the Dumpster, and back into the building. It's nice to get the chance to go outside unless it's raining. I finally reach the office by ten-thirty and toss my pile of papers on the desk. I sit down, pick up the phone, and call Chris in the kitchen. He always seems to get off the phone right after I leave the kitchen.

"What's the soup for Express?" I ask.

"Curried carrot and potato leek and Cheddar. Do we have anything on the fourteenth?"

I roll my chair to the right and look up at the three months of calendar pages on the wall.

"Not yet," I reply.

"Good. I just booked my cooking class that day. The grocery store called. They need a delivery today."

"What do they need?"

"I think they wanted ten Caesar, ten balsamics, and four tomato gingers, but I'm not positive."

"Check and let me know. Is there anything else?"

"Did you hear about Ryan yet? He got a ticket last night in New York. He was hanging out the window of a car after a Yankee game waving an Orioles T-shirt. What an idiot! Anyway, I'll be right down to do specials."

"Okay. Wait. What were those soups again?"

"Curried carrot potato—"

"Leek and Cheddar. Thanks. Bye."

I call Express next.

"Do you have everything on the special sheet from yesterday?" I ask.

"Yes."

"Did the kitchen send you anything new?"

"Yeah, I got meat loaf, but I'm out of lasagne. Oh, and I need aprons and decaf."

"All right. I'll be down in a minute."

I quickly make changes to the Express specials, start printing them, then listen to the phone messages on the answering machine. Reservations for next Tuesday and a question about catering. I scribble down the numbers and grab the special sheets from the printer, the aprons from the laundry bin, and the coffee from the cabinet. I keep the laundry in the office because the chefs would use fifty towels per person per day if I let them. At thirty cents each they can really add up. Coffee beans are also in the office because they tend to wander off when not locked up.

I walk left out of the office, down the hallway, back out of the building, and across the courtyard, where we have an outside dining area for Metro Express. I have a vague memory of what I was planning on doing today, but I can't quite remember what it was. I can't believe that Ryan didn't get shot in New York last night. I pick up a napkin, throw it away, and check to see if the tables are clean under the table mats before going downstairs into Express.

"The courtyard looks good. I've got your specials, coffee, and aprons," I say as I lay them on top of the deli case. "Do you need anything else?"

"I still need my soup, and there's water on the floor by the phone."

"Where's it coming from?"

"I don't know."

"Did you check the sump pump?"

"What?"

I examine the water on the floor and check on the pump. I run some water in the sink, flip on the breaker, and hear the pump kick in. Metro Express is now ready for service. The bread is on display, the coffee has been made, the cookies have been baked, and I am on my way back to the office. I spot the dishwasher coming through the parking lot on his way to get fresh fry oil from storage as I'm crossing the courtyard.

When I get back to the office, Chris and Jerry have settled in. Chris is at the computer pecking out the lunch specials for Metro Bis with two fingers and Jerry is asking, "What do you think we should do?"

"About what?" I ask.

"The dishwasher," Chris replies, and begins printing the special sheets.

"The person or the machine?" I ask, only half kidding.

"The machine," says Jerry. "It's been leaking, and we're waiting for the guy to come fix it."

"I was hoping he would come before lunch. We're not going to be able to do any dishes," Chris adds.

"It's leaking that bad?" I really can't afford to fix the dishwasher right now.

"It's not that bad," says Jerry. "Chicken Little is exaggerating again. We haven't leaked into the downstairs yet, and we can probably do the dishes during lunch if we keep a bucket under the machine."

As he finishes, the specials stop printing and they both get up to leave.

"Let me know what's going on," I request as they head out the door.

Chris yells from the hallway that the repairman should be in after lunch. I walk around to the other side of the desk as the phone rings. My father, our attorney, is on the other line.

"Did you get a chance to read the lease modification?" I ask.

"Yeah, everything looks fine with that. I'm calling to let you know that I got another letter from your linen company today."

"Uh-huh. What did they have to say?"

"They wanted to let me know that they are working hard to maintain the standards that are laid out in your contract."

I moan, "Why won't they just end the contract?"

"I don't think they want to, honey. Listen, we were thinking about coming for dinner tonight. Two at six o'clock?"

"Sure."

"Okay. Well. I've got to go. Take it easy. Have a good day. I'll see you later. Bye."

I attribute his brisk phone manner to his having been a divorce attorney for twenty-five years. After I hang up, I check the e-mail. Four new messages. Two are junk, one is from a friend in Tennessee, and the other's from the TV show that Chris taped last week. The host wants the recipes of the dishes. I'm just about to call Chris upstairs when the phone rings. It's Express, and it's busy.

I race back down the hall, outside, across the courtyard, and into the entryway of Express, where six people are crammed. I wait on the next three people and take a phone order. One wants a turkey wrap with bacon, bean sprouts, roasted red-pepper hummus, and romaine instead of spinach, the next wants the veggie wrap with no cheese and a baby-green salad, and the third is allergic to citrus and garlic. What can she eat? We settle on cranberry-stuffed chicken with whipped potatoes. After all the waiting customers have gotten their lunches, I make two pesto chicken wraps, one Caesar chicken wrap, and a spinach salad, and pack a pint of udon noodles for the phone order. I put away the bean sprouts, the chicken, and the lettuces and refill the udon noodle bowl from the supply underneath the deli case. I wipe down the counter and head back to the office.

While I am unlocking the door, I can hear the intercom from the restaurant ringing. I race for the phone and knock a pile of cookbooks onto the floor.

"Where have you been?" demands Chris. "We need help up here. We're getting spanked."

As I run (they never call unless they really, really need help) past the office display window, I catch my reflection in the glass. I probably should have ironed my shirt this morning. It looks as if I pulled it off the floor of the backseat of my car. I also notice the wry smile. Who would have thought I would have ended up here?

26

KRAFT MAC AND CHEESE, BUTTERED NOODLES WITH HOT DOGS, AND MARSHMALLOW FLUFF VERSUS COQ AU VIN, SCHNITZEL WITH SPAETZLE, AND MARZIPAN

*M*y mother was shocked. "*You are dating a chef? That's such a waste. I should be the one dating a chef. At least I like food.*" Clearly the irony had not been lost on her, and I couldn't blame her for being surprised. I was the kind of kid whose friends' parents used to call my mother when I was playing at their house. "Mary Jane, I can't find anything to feed your daughter. What will this kid eat?" It actually wasn't that hard to feed me. My favorite dishes were cheeseburgers and hot dogs with buttered noodles. In an emergency, I would also eat grilled cheese and popcorn.

When I was young my mother was a health-food nut, and she was determined to feed me a well-balanced diet. For an after-school snack I always got a glass of 1 percent milk and an apple. I still hate apples unless they're baked with lots of sugar. After I complained about the apple for ten or fifteen minutes, she would give me a rice cake and the dreaded jar of all-natural peanut butter. I never really understood natural peanut butter. What was that liquid on the top? Why did it have to be mixed? The peanut butter at my friends' houses never had to be mixed, and they got cookies as a snack after school. Hungry, I would slide the knife through the upper two inches of oil into the thick, hard peanut paste at the bottom. After several unsuccessful, thrusting attempts, I would usually give up and ask for the jelly. If the peanut butter jar was half empty, I might be more successful and manage to get a glob of runny nuts onto the Styrofoam cracker. I begged my mother to buy the real peanut butter I knew existed, but she wouldn't give in.

She also stood firm on whole-wheat bread with crust. I hated the cardboardlike texture, with strange bumpy grains that begged to be picked out, and longed for those occasional trips to my grandmother's house. Her bread was closer to white. I think it must have been light wheat, but, more important, she cut off the edges. My grandfather always gave me a hard time, but you could tell that he was happy to get the extra crust.

This obsession with bread peaked with my favorite field

trip in elementary school. Other kids loved the Bronx Zoo, the circus, Mystic Aquarium, or the Snow White play at the Bushnell Theater in Hartford. My favorite trip was to the Wonder Bread factory. All of my classmates paraded single-file past all the machinery, conveyor belts, mixers, slicers, and ovens. The warm, moist, sweet air was intoxicating. At the end of the day, we each got a free loaf of precious bread to take home. I was so excited. I thought that that one little loaf would last forever, like the gobstopper candy in *Willy Wonka and the Chocolate Factory*. I would never have to eat that chunky brown bread ever again. Imagine my dismay when I accidentally sat on my immortal loaf on the bus ride home. Even when I burst into the house sobbing with my bag of mutilated bread, my mother refused to buy a new, pure white loaf. "It's even forced with vitamins," I whimpered.

At some point my mother must have given in. Maybe she was tired of the little white worms in our kitchen cabinets that lived off the organic grains, cereals, and flour that she bought. (I swear those worms found a way to move from house to house each time we did, and I still can't even look at, much less eat, an English muffin without recalling the terror of tearing one open and watching the worms quickly choosing between the halves.) It could have been my relentless demands for Marshmallow Fluff and Froot Loops, but it was probably just the added pressure from my brother and sister. The chorus of the three of us singing the Coke theme song at the top of our lungs in the grocery store while we hid junk food in the bottom of the basket must have done her in.

My mother may have bought more "crap" (as she called it) than she wanted to, but she still managed to serve a meat-potato-vegetable family meal at the dinner table every day as I grew into early adolescence. I ate a ton of potatoes, did my best to avoid the vegetables, and spent no less than twenty minutes dissecting the unidentifiable meat. At dinner I would examine the meat and prep the flesh for surgery. I inspected all sides to determine the best approach necessary to eliminate all of the inedible parts. All remaining fat, sinew, gristle, veins, and discoloration was carefully removed prior to consumption. I used to drive my mother insane. She always compared me to her seventy-year-old aunt, who picked at her food like a bird. "Just eat it already!" My mother insisted that I was being ridiculous, but deep down she must have had hopes that her daughter would become a brain surgeon.

I was her complete opposite. She ate absolutely everything that I didn't want to even touch with a fork. I could never understand her desire for dark chicken meat, which I had eliminated from my diet due to its color. I was particularly revolted by her need to chew on the chicken's bones. She would gnaw at the meatless bone for three or four minutes, the cartilage and ligaments snapping loudly under the pressure of her teeth.

"Oh my God, you are so gross," I would say.

"What?" she would ask, puzzled and offended.

Chicken for dinner was okay because I knew what kind of meat it was and what parts I needed to avoid. My parents called almost every meat but chicken "pork." I wasn't sure what pork was or what animal it came from, and I had no idea that my dinner had come from our backyard.

My parents kept lambs and pigs when I was growing up, and if the wind blew in just the right direction, you could enjoy the stench from the top of the swimming pool slide. At the end of each summer, a farmer would drive his truck up to the small pen and take the animals away "for the winter." One year my mother ended up riding a pig as she attempted to coax it into the truck. That pig wasn't stupid. He knew where he was going even if I had no clue. A little while after the animals' departure, our extra freezer in the entryway would be filled with taped brown-paper packages. I even went one year to the farm with my mother to pick them up. For some reason I never made the connection. But I also believed in Santa Claus until I was twelve.

All winter long my mother would serve what she called "pork" from those packages in the freezer. I didn't realize that "pork" actually was pig and often lamb. I can't blame her for not telling us. She watched us bottle-feed the animals each spring.

After my mother finally agreed to buy most of the junk food that we requested (I don't think she ever recovered from the Christmas when I asked my aunt for Coke as a gift), I delivered another blow when I announced I was a vegetarian my senior year in high school. I'm sure that she wasn't surprised, but she was pretty annoyed. She was still attempting that "balanced meal" thing that I never understood. When my brother and sister followed my lead, she made a valiant attempt to create healthy vegetarian meals.

Before I made my announcement, I was eating mostly potatoes at home and Burger King double cheeseburgers with large fries and Cokes in the car. I ate a lot of pizza, too. (Ask my mother about my youthful interaction with the famed fast food. She'll roll her eyes and talk about years when I only ate the topping, then I only ate the crust, and finally I ate the whole damn thing at once. I went through phases with the tops and bottoms of asparagus and broccoli, too.) For a snack in the afternoon after high school my brother and I would microwave a block of preservative-packed mozzarella and eat it with our hands while watching TV. It was a lot better than the rice cakes, and it was fun to eat.

Until the day the school nurse announced that the health center would be conducting cholesterol readings during lunch, I never considered that my hard-won eating habits could be affecting my body. All I had to do was show up, get a finger pricked, and they'd give me a number. There were two sophomore boys ahead of me. The nurse took a finger prick from each of us. The first boy's results came back at 115. The second boy came in at 103. The first boy had his blood drawn again to see if he could beat the second boy.

The nurse took me aside to tell me my cholesterol number: 175. That's when I discovered pasta and salad, the two main staples of my diet today.

Since I was giving my meat-free diet a try, I ate a lot of SpaghettiOs before my tastes matured to Kraft macaroni and cheese. I later progressed to Pasta Roni and ramen noodles in college.

By the time I met Chris, I should have been brined by the enormous amount of salt that I ingested each day. I have no idea how he tolerated me. He never said a word when I insisted that we eat mozzarella sticks in Friendly's. He never got upset in the beginning of our relationship when we couldn't dine in any upscale restaurants because there was nothing on the menu that I would look at, much less ingest. Eventually, with careful persistence, he convinced me that I would find something to eat, and we would go out to regular restaurants. Chris would just watch quietly while I enjoyed a bowl of whipped potatoes with a side of steamed spinach. But he crossed the line when he talked me into a sushi bar. I watched in terror, groaned with disgust, and sipped chilled water while he downed a whole baby octopus.

It never really occurred to me how different our culinary experiences had been until one night when we were eating pizza. A food writer friend of Chris's had asked him about food memories, and he wanted a list of all the dishes that Chris associated with happy thoughts. While we waited for our pizza, Chris studiously recorded all of the foods on both sides of a bar napkin until he ran out of space. He paused for a moment when he had finished, tilted his head, looked at me, and said, "Bill says I'm an anomaly and that not everyone has great food memories."

For him food is a passionate, interesting, fun, and comforting adventure. Chris told me about waking up early on Sundays to go to a chicken farm. Once there, he and his brothers would pick out the perfect breakfast eggs. They carefully carried them home, whipped them individually, and enjoyed them. My earliest egg experience involved force and threats. I would sit for hours in a stiff ladder-back kitchen chair hoping that my parents would give in and free me from the table. When this didn't happen I decided that I would drown the egg with ketchup. Once the now-cold egg was fully eclipsed by the red mass, I choked it back.

Chris grew up in Forest Hills, New York, right next to the city in a mostly Jewish neighborhood. When he had money he would walk down the street to one of the many Jewish markets and buy a fat, salty kosher pickle. The store clerk allowed Chris to put his sweaty little hand in the five-gallon barrel and pull out his very own pickle. When he got a little older, the clerk let him use the tongs to pry the best pickle from the depths of the bucket. All the way back home Chris would crunch on a pickle as big as his hand. If he had extra money, he would buy a knish and eat that on the way home, too. When I had money I bought Tootsie Rolls and Fireballs. In the summer he and his mom walked down the street to a field where blackberries grew. They ate the sun-warmed berries all afternoon, then went home to wash their juice-stained hands. I picked blackberries, too, when my parents made me. We used to sell them in front of the house. Some woman would order four quarts on a ninety-five-degree day, and I would head into the patch to fill the containers while my brother swam in the pool.

All right, I do have good food memories, too. My mother taught me how to make meat loaf and real macaroni and cheese. I loved decorating gingerbread cookies and making popcorn balls. But Chris has no bad food memories, and there are only a few things that he won't eat: mayonnaise, yogurt, and cauliflower. My list is endless. Chris's experiences have always been enriching, sensual, and fun. He has a respect for food that I will never fully understand.

It might have something to do with my parents' treatment of food. One sweltering summer evening my parents were preparing to go out, and my brother was playing in the muddy sandbox out back. I said something to antagonize him and was soon running for my life from a mud pie that was destined to fly. I zigzagged around trees, and up and down the driveway, and when I noticed that he wasn't tiring, I wisely bolted for the front door. The steps to the house slowed me down, as did flinging open the screen—he had gotten close enough to take a shot. As he reached the top of the stairs, he took aim. I hung a quick right to get to the locked protection of my bedroom. That mud pie flew through the swinging screen door. It aerodynamically sailed like no pie had a right to over the kitchen table. It slid past my confused, frozen father, and it landed with a loud *plunk* in the vigorously boiling spaghetti about to be strained for dinner. Time was running short, the baby-sitter (the poor, poor baby-sitter) would be arriving shortly, and we were to be fed beforehand. My mother walked into the kitchen while my father stirred the dirty pasta water.

"Look what your son did!" my father yelled.

"It could be worse," she said.

"How?"

"He could have gotten the mud in the sauce."

My father strained, washed, and rinsed the spaghetti as well as it would allow and served it while my mother finished blow-drying her hair. I can still feel that gritty pasta against my teeth and remember my skin crawling.

I asked Chris if his parents would have served this pasta delicacy to him and his brothers. He paused and said gravely, "There would never have been any dirt in the pasta."

Chris remembers sitting in fancy restaurants as a child with a napkin on his lap and his fork and knife properly in hand. I remember my brother flinging strands of spaghetti around in a circle above his head before letting them go flying off into the dining room. There would have never been any dirt in Chris's parents' pasta because they were much stricter with their children and had instilled in them a respect for food very early on.

To Chris's family there is nothing better than a freshly killed goose (bonus if you're the one who gets the shot), funky aged cheeses, handmade spaetzle, and vegetables from their enormous garden. Chris's mother, Gertie, has a compost pile the size of a small hill. Her favorite gift from me was a morel mushroom spore starter that she planted in her compost. I don't think that it ever spawned, but the thought of fresh mushrooms delighted her.

Gertie went to culinary school in Austria and worked as a restaurant manager in New York City before moving permanently to Goshen, Connecticut, where she makes wedding cakes and pastries for all of the famous people with homes in the country. Chris's father, Paul, is a pastry chef who worked for Marriott for twenty years before retiring to a second job teaching at the Culinary Institute of America in Hyde Park, New York. At one point Paul ran his own pastry shop in the Marriott-owned Essex House. He made the best croissants and truffles in the city, according to Chris, who used to eat at the shop regularly until he grew so tired of sweets that he still doesn't really enjoy them.

I will forever be a mystery to Chris's family. They just don't understand my relationship with food, and no one can blame them. It took no less than five years before Chris's dad stopped pulling out a wineglass from the cabinet for me. His mother still slides hard-won items across the table— "You eat this?" I know that it can't be easy to find quality foie gras in a jar, but I just can't eat it. There are cultural differences, too. Whenever we leave Chris's parents' house, we are laden with a variety of items, from chocolate truffles to homemade pickles and clothing that Chris will never fit in again. It must be a European thing, a way to clean out your house without throwing anything away.

Gertie used to intimidate me with her Austrian accent and abrupt behavior, but I've realized that we are a lot more alike than I would have thought. She is unusually active. In the summer Gertie plants, weeds, cuts, and trims. In the fall she harvests, cans, bottles, and preserves. In the winter she helps with the Special Olympics ski team.

The first couple of years we visited Chris's parents, they used to annoy me. Gertie never stops moving. She won't even sit down to have a conversation. All visiting hours are spent perched on a backless stool on either side of a counter in, of course, the kitchen. "Why can't we sit on the couch?" I would whine to Chris on the way home. "It's just not right," he would reply. At some point it all made sense; they are restaurant people. They can't stay still and I have much more in common with them than I'd like to admit. I now prepare myself for three hours of sensory overload, and I sit on one of the kitchen table chairs instead. Gertie reaches in and out of the fridge, serves us a special cheese (it's special because she limits Paul's intake when his cholesterol gets too high), makes ice cream, and continues to prepare dinner. She's always working on dinner, and it doesn't matter what time of day it is. Paul pulls out three wineglasses and makes

Chris select a bottle from the dusty, never-temperature-controlled wine rack. Chris pours the wine while Paul drags me to the computer in his office off of the dining area. I love to go to their home. It's like being the most popular kids on the playground. The two of them fight for my attention, Chris's attention, and both of us at the same time. It's funny to hear Gertie in the kitchen shouting to Chris (who is two feet away) about pumpkin seed oil from her hometown of Gras, Austria. In the next room, Paul will be showing me pictures of my niece on the computer. Gertie brings the oil and Chris into the office to gain the spotlight, then rushes out to the garage to grab her homemade raspberry wine before she loses anyone's attention. My mother sprouted an avocado pit once.

Not surprisingly, Chris found his way to a professional kitchen much sooner than I did, and he can't even remember his first impressions, he was so young. I can't imagine what the Essex House kitchen must have looked like to a four-year-old. I vaguely remember the first time I was in a restaurant kitchen. It looked enormous to me. I was in seventh or eighth grade and one of my friends' parents owned an independent quick-service joint in Southington, Connecticut, called Dan's Top Dog. It was a huge kitchen compared with mine at home. I could actually stand inside the refrigerator; it was an entire room. I was also captivated by the soda dispenser. All I had to do was put the cup underneath and press a button. The machine knew how much soda fit in the cup and would automatically stop when it was full. My friend was not at all interested and couldn't understand my obsession with the griddle, where twenty-five burgers could be cooked at once. She had already started working for her parents and would have preferred to be a customer. We would sit in the plastic booths and eat French fries while she impatiently waited to be driven home.

I would have never dreamed of running a restaurant when I was that young. Chris, on the other hand, could picture it but wanted nothing to do with it even though he worked in restaurants throughout his teen years. After he scored high on the math portion of his SATs in high school, the guidance counselor recommended that he pursue a career in electrical engineering. Chris dropped out after three and a half years, one term short of graduation, after realizing his life would consist of creating systems on papers but never building them. So he went to the Culinary Institute of America like the rest of the family.

ONCE UPON
A BRINE

I applied for my first food-service job at the end of my senior year of high school. My dad set it up. His secretary's husband owned a restaurant and an ice cream shop. I went to see the restaurant after school one day dressed in a skirt and a button-down shirt, the required uniform for school. The owner looked skeptically at me. No one had ever applied in a skirt before and had only wanted to work on the weekends. He wasn't sure whether to hire me despite my referral. He carefully looked me over and was relieved when he saw my hands.

"It's good that a girl like you doesn't have fingernails," he said.

"Why?" I wondered.

"They break easily," he snorted.

"The women or the nails?"

I got the job and began work in the ice cream shop three days later. In my unscheduled free time I tried to work in the kitchen of the owner's restaurant across the street, hoping to be a prep cook. I wanted to be there because everyone joked with one another and had fun doing their jobs. Service was a period of intense activity that required concentration, organization, and determination. It was much more exciting than scooping ice cream. There was a mission to be accomplished in the kitchen and a gratifying sense of accomplishment at the end of the night. The stress level ran high, and it seemed as if the world might come to an end if the food didn't reach the plate in time. I loved the pulse of the kitchen, but I really didn't belong there. I am still slow and sloppy with prep work. I'm sure that the owner kept me in the kitchen for entertainment, not production. He would hand me a bag of spinach and tell me to sort out all of the bad pieces.

"How do I know if they're bad?"

"Just pick out any of the pieces that you wouldn't eat." I threw out half of the bag of spinach. He stared, unbelievingly.

"Why did you throw all of that away?"

"You told me to throw out what I wouldn't eat."

"Maybe you should just throw out what normal people won't eat, like the ones that have large brown spots like this one."

I pulled the spinach from the trash to be resorted and washed.

My most famous incident in that kitchen was the first time that I cleaned romaine lettuce. I wanted to be like one of the guys, so I grabbed a five-gallon bucket, pushed the always helpful Ecuadorians out of the way, filled the container to the brim, and hoisted it to the prep table. I tore out the stem from each romaine leaf and placed it in my full bucket of water. I was so proud to finally be doing something right, until the owner walked by and pushed my floating lettuce down into the overfull bucket.

"It's hot!" he shrieked.

I pretended that I didn't know the water was hot. I said that the Ecuadorians had filled the bucket for me. He knew that I was lying. The Ecuadorians would never put hot water in the bucket for the lettuce. The kitchen made fun of me all the time during the next couple of weeks. I finally asked a friend why hot water was so bad. "The lettuce wilts, silly." I had thought that hot water made everything cleaner.

Most of the time I was in the ice cream shop with dry, sticky remnants stuck to the skin between my elbow and my wrist. The owner's nephew worked Saturday nights with me during the summer, and I would squeeze around his large body in the tiny store to make milk shakes and banana splits. The owner's sister was in charge of the ice cream shop, and she was anal retentive about cleanliness, which I learned to value later. I swept carefully every day (she left pennies in the corners to make sure that everything was clean); I mopped faithfully because I never wanted to disappoint her. While I sat on the stool waiting for customers in the afternoon, I looked out across the street at the restaurant and wondered what was going on. Sometimes the owner would take me on caterings, if the event didn't conflict with my ice cream shop schedule. I had so much fun going to other people's houses, arranging appetizers on plates, and ransacking their drawers for spoons. When I left for my first year of college after that summer, I knew that I would be back, and I hoped to win a more prestigious position.

At college in Pennsylvania I realized that I would need a weekend job if I planned on paying my phone bill each month. I applied at the bar in the center of town that served real food and carded their customers before letting them drink. There was another bar down the street where all of the younger students drank, but I didn't want to work in a place where I didn't feel safe. I was hired at the first place as a buser and hostess for Friday night, Saturday night, and Sunday lunch. I made $2.63 an hour and got tipped twenty dollars per shift if I didn't anger the waitstaff. They had sections and always felt that I was favoring one person over another when I cleared and sat tables. I was just trying to put customers on tables, and I never knew who had which section. The work was okay, and I was finally on the floor in a real restaurant job.

My big break came on a Sunday morning. I had left the night before when the dining room closed at ten o'clock. The kitchen was supposed to stay open until midnight, serving the bar customers. I had been working for only five weeks and didn't realize that the kitchen staff consisted of men from the local jail's work release program. These guys were allowed out during the day to work and went back to jail at night to sleep. The Sunday I came in was chaos. The owner had gotten in a fight with the kitchen employees the night before, and they had all walked out around eleven o'clock. We were about to open for lunch and the kitchen staff hadn't come to work. When the owner asked if any of the waitstaff had any kitchen experience, I was bold enough to raise my hand. I had only done a little prep work and tagged along on some caterings, but I figured that it couldn't be that hard to work in the kitchen. The owner, a high-school kid I had never seen before, and I walked into the kitchen. The three of us would be doing lunch today. I was a little disappointed to be assigned to the salad and appetizer station, but I hoped that I would be allowed to cook the half-pound hamburgers if I proved myself capable.

The first tickets rolled in slowly at the beginning of the 150-person lunch. I grabbed a plastic-coated menu from the hostess station and went to work. My station was already set up, so I just took what I needed and assembled each dish as well as I could. I had seen most of the items while working on the floor over the last few weeks. I was doing all right until I got an order for a Reuben. The menu was pretty vague about this sandwich, and I had never seen one before, so I needed to call for help. As the owner explained the mystery of the Reuben, the printer started to spew tickets. I couldn't believe that eight orders could come in one after another like that. I hung them all in front of me and made each item on each ticket in order. It would have made sense to make three orders of mozzarella sticks at once, instead of

running back and forth to the freezer every two minutes—
but what did I know? The owner was in the weeds (totally
behind) with hamburgers and didn't notice that I was getting behind until well-done burgers were up in the window
and the waitstaff were waiting for my veggie platters. He
jumped over to my side to bail me out, but I kept on going.

Even after I mastered the Reuben, grilled cheese was a
problem. I rolled the bread on a metal container filled with
butter, placed it on the flat top, put down the cheese, and
burned the sandwich. Every time. I couldn't figure out how
to turn down the griddle, so I came up with a new technique:
I buttered the bread, toasted it properly, took it off the heat,
put on the cheese, and popped it in the microwave. Why else
was the microwave there? The bread didn't look so great
after the cheese was melted, so I put it back on the flat top.
No one sent the grilled cheese back, so I guess that it was
edible. I'm sure people could tell that something was not
quite right when they ate it, but it would be hard to determine exactly what was wrong.

When I dropped one of the cheese sandwiches on the
floor just as the owner was screaming for it, I froze and
looked at him.

"Pick it up!" he bellowed.

I wasn't about to mention that it was on the ground. I had
just learned what some kitchen employees call the three-
second rule (or the five-second rule or the ten-second rule,
depending on how long it takes to pick something up). The

theory is that the item is hot enough when it hits the floor to kill all of the bacteria if you pick it up quickly. It turns out that the rule applies only in restaurants that have absolutely no regard for the public-health codes. The grilled cheese "sandwich" and five-second rule (I was a little slow) aside, by the end of the shift I could fill a broccoli and cheese potato skin without having to look at the menu. (It was my first shift, I wasn't that bright.) And I must have done all right despite my vegetable pita pocket filled with the carrot and celery sticks for the buffalo wings (I guess I should have chopped the vegetables so they fit in the bread) because I was freed from the floor. I had graduated to the other side of the swinging doors.

When I came to work my station the next weekend, the work release program was back in business. Since I was the only woman in the kitchen, the inmates leered at me throughout service, making rude remarks. I was the Fry-O-Lator girl and had to cross over to their side of the line to drop fries under the heat lamp. They all called me "the fry girl," which I took as a compliment. At least I wasn't a buser anymore. Not that it made a difference. The place was a dump. I never wanted to eat in restaurants again after I worked there. Thankfully, it burned to the ground several years ago. I can just picture all of the cockroaches scattering in the flames.

I had never seen cockroaches before working in that kitchen and was surprised that they would come out during the day. I often worried about stepping on a pregnant one and tracking her evil offspring back to my college dorm. It's no wonder that they were everywhere. I quickly learned that the Dumpster was kept inside the building at the end of a concrete ramp. (Chris says this is common in cities, but I had never seen garbage inside a restaurant before, either.) The experience has forever made me worry about water in metal pans. I used to make Kate, my college roommate, crazy by enforcing the drying of all pots thoroughly before they were put away. I can still remember reaching for the square metal containers we used to store the food in at the end of the night, only to find them filled with drinking cockroaches.

The other problem was the employees. They were thrilled to be out of jail for a few hours and couldn't have cared less about the food. All night long they would walk to the bar for rum and Cokes. The bartender eventually gave them their own bottle to keep by the soda dispenser to guarantee that her food orders would reach the bar. Since their goal was to get hammered every night, and feeding the customers was only a byproduct, the food on the floor in the kitchen was two to three inches thick. French fries, burgers, lettuce, chicken, rolls—at least one of each menu item found its way to the floor. The three-second rule didn't matter to them because none of them cared how long it took to put the food out. Considering how drunk everyone was by the end of the shift, it was a miracle that anything made it to a plate.

The food on the floor of my side of the line was especially deep despite my uniquely sober status. I had to make nachos, grande and regular. It all started with a plate. I piled chips on the plate, then layered a black-bean mixture and cheese on top. More chips and more cheese, then into the oven. It doesn't sound that hard. But the chips never settled. They slipped off of the plate as I walked from the shelf to the soup warmer of black beans. Then it was back to the line for cheese, with chips fighting to escape from the heavy beans to become cockroach food. I added another layer of chips. There simply wasn't enough room on the plate. I went back to the line. It was like running a race with a full-to-the-brim martini glass. I crammed on the cheese and slung the plate into the convection oven. About half of the chips from the bag lay on the floor. That was okay, though. It was much better to think that the crunching below my feet was chips.

Sometimes the roaches got lost and ended up in the dining room. Customers lucky enough to spot them got a free entrée, but the drinks were never on the house. Sometimes there were bar fights and the front window would be broken when I came to work the next day. I would still like to hunt down and kill the guy who programmed the jukebox to play "Cheeseburger in Paradise" thirty-five times in a row. Still, I would have kept the job except that one of my friends was sleeping with the owner. His wife didn't really appreciate the relationship, didn't want me around to remind her of it, so she made it difficult for me until I left. I got up at five A.M. and delivered seventy-seven newspapers a day instead.

I was glad to get back to my summer job when the school year ended. The little restaurant with the ice cream shop had expanded to 120 seats, and I had been promoted to hostess on the weekends. I still scooped ice cream during the week, which is when I encountered Chris and his olives. After I had been home for a few weeks of summer break, I found myself inexplicably drawn to him. During the first few months of our relationship (you don't really "date" a chef because of the schedule he keeps) I watched him cook dinner for forty people with a chubby-cheeked Ecuadorian named Santiago. When I was tired of watching, I went home and wrote about him:

Rhythmic grace. Fluidity of movement. Intense concentration. Respect of materials. Paying attention to everything that goes on but seems to be involved in his own world. Looks at me and a smile of recognition appears. He is propelled back to reality. Like a child learning to play with a chemistry set. Touching and tasting everything. Looking at a consommé curiously to see how it will come out. The wonder of food. A complete grasp and the knowledge of what to expect. The joy of discovering or creating something new. A "bitching consommé."

A disorderly scattered appearance. Looks slightly burnt and aged but with a creative vitality. Slightly silly in chef pants, clogs, a soiled coat, apron down to his ankles, a black back brace to "hold his body together" for two extra hours, hair too long and unruly with a hat that only makes it worse, and a pair of glasses to match his mood. "It's Sunday, and it doesn't matter what I look like. It's a miracle that I'm even here."

Precision. Gliding hands. Dancing eyes. Controlled. Calm. Collected. Patient. Playfully daring with a dash of humor. The courage to dream and the motivation, persistence, and perseverance to capture it. The freedom of creation. He makes me potatoes with a smiling garnish. Two eyes of scallion, a tomato nose, and carrot mouth.

He never gets angry when something comes out wrong. He just does it again. "I've been working on pastrami for three years now. It never comes out exactly how I want it. There's still something missing."

He can't drive by fruit stands in the summer. He has to stop and see what's in season locally. Needs to feel the fruit and smell the vegetables.

Treats people as he treats food. Some food he is gentle and careful with, and other things he just cuts up and tosses aside.

Caught up in an energy that won't let him stop. It pushes him through the day.

"I like to keep six things going at once. I don't feel comfortable without everything going. As soon as one thing ends I start something else."

He fascinated me. If I stood in the right place in the entryway while hostessing on Saturday night, I could see him working the line in the kitchen. I loved working with him. No one knew that we were seeing each other, and he eventually let me roll gnocchi instead of pitting olives. I used to hang out at night in the bar upstairs watching him with his sous-chef. They would drink from three glasses until they went home. Coffee, tequila, and sparkling water filled the table. If he got a day off (there weren't very many back then because the restaurant had just opened), we would drive around Litchfield County. He always stopped at farm stands, new restaurants, and bakeries. I went along to watch, but we mostly worked. I had transferred to a school in Connecticut and when I went back to school in the fall, I stayed with Chris and kept on hostessing on the weekends.

I hardly ever watch him cook now like I did then. We still go on food-related trips on our days off, but I'm much too busy to hang out in the kitchen. Sometimes I stop by a familiar table on a Friday night, and they ask me to recommend one of the specials. I stall and try to read the specials upside down and inside out while they hold the list in their hands. I see opah; that's a good fish flown in fresh from New Zealand. Sometimes there's an ingredient that I don't recognize, so I have to run back to the kitchen and ask. They usually make fun of me. "Sea beans? Sea beans have been on the menu for two weeks. Where have you been?" I smile and rush back to the table with the explanation.

In college I would have never asked the kitchen about an ingredient. I was way too cocky. After all, I had worked as the fry girl during the previous school year. I was an expert. When the owner of the 120-seat restaurant and ice cream shop decided to expand business by opening a banquet facility, I went along while Chris stayed at the restaurant. I catered for about a year and developed an intense dislike of brides.

While I was surviving brides on the weekends, I finished my degree in English and secondary education. I found that I enjoyed catering more than I liked school. A part of Chris must have rubbed off on me, just as my mother had hoped it would. I first realized I had been permeated by Chris's chefdom and might be on my way to a life in the restaurant business while dining with Kate. We were eating baby-green salads, a huge transformation for someone who only ate iceberg, then only ate the hearts of the romaine lettuce, but during this meal I had progressed to a variety of field greens. I had encountered them only during the last six months, and when I did, Chris proceeded to identify each and every leaf. The weeds weren't so foreign after all. I had eaten beet greens before, and when I ate each leaf separately, they weren't that bad. But Kate and I were enjoying full-blown baby-green salads with all the leaves mixed together. In the middle of a conversation about the lameness of the O. J. Simpson trial, I paused and said, "Have you heard about the baby-green movement in the United States?"

Kate froze with fork in midflight and stared at me. Then she shrieked with laughter. "The baby-green movement? Ooh, no. Tell me more."

How could I have gone from iceberg to the farming of baby greens in such a short time? By now I had realized that I didn't really want to teach despite my degree, so I kept on working at the banquet facility while I pondered the rest of my life. In the late fall after my graduation, I ran into my high-school headmistress and she insisted that I call the school and apply for an assistant librarian position. It was perfect timing, since the frequency of banquets in Connecticut decreases between "leaf-peeping" time and Christmas parties.

I didn't see Chris as much when I worked at the library. I was always up before him, and he was always up after me. I realized after a while that I could take naps in the afternoon and be able to see him at night. It was while I was working at this job that he decided it was time to open his own restaurant. I say *his* because he didn't want me to have any part of it. He wanted me to pursue my own dreams. I didn't really have any career dreams, so I figured I'd find out what he was up to.

I never thought of owning a restaurant until Chris talked about his goal of owning one. He told me the best restaurants in the country are now chef owned. At the time I had no idea what the best restaurants could possibly be, but it seemed most likely to be true. The chef is the most vital ingredient in the restaurant. They set a certain standard and style. A chef can hire people to run the floor, do the books, and promote the business. He can replace these employees if necessary and the restaurant will not falter during the change. An owner who is not a chef is always risking the loss of that main employee. If the chef leaves, the menu needs to be changed, and someone needs to quickly fill that role without the customers noticing. Problem is chefs are always leaving, and star chefs are big news. Everyone wants to know the chef. The restaurant owner who is not a chef needs to promote an image rather than a person, and an image is much harder to market. He needs to define a concept, explain why it is unique and better, and give it a name. A chef just stands tall and says, "This is me. This is the cooking of Fred. I am Fred. This is my food." It's not ever that easy, but the chef is a concrete concept that people can see and understand. Upscale, modern Northern Italian cuisine served in a hip, young, casual setting is much more difficult to promote.

Chris wanted to own a restaurant because he wanted the creative control that he lacked while employed by others. He knew that he was the most essential ingredient, and he didn't have to have a marketing gimmick to sell his food. I really wanted to help him achieve his dreams, I already had some restaurant experience, and I knew that we had nothing to lose.

Finding a restaurant took a lot of time. I decided to quit doing banquet service and get a waitressing job while working at my high-school library. This way I could make more money and learn more about restaurant service. I ended up at a Swiss and Austrian restaurant with traditional service, calves' brains, and every cut of veal possible. It sickened me. I hated to go into the walk-in refrigerator for fear that I might discover a live cow waiting to be slaughtered. The specialty of the place was Kalbshaxen, a shank of veal carved from the bone tableside. People loved it, and I liked to recommend the beast because it was always good to score brownie points with the chef. The meat was held up with an aluminum foil form and carried high through the dining room. A tray stand was set before the table and the tray displayed on top. The show began with a knife. I would separate the meat from the bone, slice it in half where it had been adhered, and then cut each piece into four round slices. Then, in true, classic Russian service, I would chase green beans around the platter with a fork and spoon in one hand. Eventually the sliced meat, beans, and the forgiving tomatoes would be placed neatly on the plate and served to the diner.

Sometimes I would raise the tray to my shoulder and return to the kitchen with no interference, other times the table would request the bone for their dogs, but the most frightening people asked for the bone on the plate. They treated me with kind disdain. Clearly I didn't know what I was doing. Why would I wander off with the bone? More important, what did they want the bone for? I could wrap it in the kitchen for their dogs. They didn't have to keep it on the plate. I never had time to see what those strange people did with the bone. I was way too busy. The chef insisted that the waitstaff make the salads and the desserts. At the beginning of service we pruned the green beans and peeled potatoes before our first tables. Not knowing exactly why the customer wanted the bone, you can't imagine my surprise when a gentle woman asked me for a marrow spoon.

"Excuse me?"

"A marrow spoon," she repeated.

I took a slow breath and asked a manager. Thankfully we did not have a marrow spoon. I certainly didn't want to encourage such a vile act. What could be more disturbing than a woman sucking the very life from a six-inch calves' thigh bone? What exactly was marrow, and why, why, why would anyone want to eat it? Chris just laughed.

"It's not that bad."

"They are sucking the new blood cells out of the bone. They are literally drinking blood. They are vampires. How can you tell me it isn't that bad? It is absolutely vile. I can think of nothing worse."

"That's because you weren't raised on offal."

"What's awful?"

"Offal. It's all the organ meats of the animal. Like the brains, liver, kidneys, and tongue that you already serve. I was raised on the stuff."

Even though I really enjoyed wearing the traditional Austrian dirndl dress with my chest hiked up to my neck, I was glad when I left to help Chris open his restaurant. The thought of chopping off the head, removing the tail, and deboning another poached trout at a table was enough to make me want to do dishes for the next six months.

Doing dishes would have been a lot easier. We had decided that we would get married on Block Island that May before the busy season. A year earlier Chris and I had flown to the island from Connecticut in a plane the size of a Volkswagen Bug with wings. We took a taxi (bigger than the plane) to the hotel. Chris had to use his sous-chef's credit card to check in because he didn't have one himself. When we got to the room, I looked out over the yard below. Chris scanned the horizon, too.

"Emus!" he shouted, and ran for the door. I hesitated and followed slowly.

"Come on," he urged. We rushed to the fenced field.

"Just look at those emus. They make the best low-fat burgers. Better than ostrich." They looked like grass huts with legs and necks to me. "You can't imagine the size of the eggs they lay," he continued. "Huge omelettes. Huge."

I smiled as I thought of my mother freaking out in Connecticut, convinced that I was engaging in premarital sin, while what I was actually doing was watching emus strut the hillside next to the hotel.

The year passed quickly and we were soon married on Block Island. I was a psychotic bride. The kind I had learned to hate while working weddings. We started planning a year before the event. I did everything. Dresses, tuxedoes, photographer, flowers, the band, the hotel rooms, the vows, everything. Without realizing it, I was on my way to becoming a restaurant owner. The wedding was just a dry run. It began with a six-course wine-tasting rehearsal dinner and ended with Wednesday-morning brunch after the wedding. It took so much planning because I hate weddings. I wanted everything to be better than perfect. I didn't want a flower-tossing, glass-clinking, garter-pulling wedding. I'd rather not get married at all than live through another stereotypical wedding from hell. I wanted floating candles that would burn for six hours. I found the candle holders in Washington, D.C., and the candles in California. There was rosemary in the wedding bouquet and the corsages. The guests signed a painting of a chef with a bride. My mother made my niece (the most unwilling flower girl) a dress from the same material as the bridesmaids' gowns. My place cards were personalized notes to each of the invited guests. I scheduled Chris for a manicure. I had both sets of parents renew their vows, and I read a poem to mark the occasion. Prior to the wedding I had sent the guests a packet of information on the island so they could entertain themselves during their free time. I also included an itinerary of recreational activities in their rooms that I had booked for them. I greeted each and every single ferry that arrived on the island during those two glorious days and helped all the guests carry their luggage to their rooms. It's a miracle that

I didn't go insane. I filled the flowerpots that I had brought with sand from the beach for the lanterns. I designed, printed, and bound the color program for the ceremony. I forced some poor pastry chef to make twenty-five individual wedding cakes to be shared between each couple that attended that blessed day. No cheesy cake-cutting, frosting-smothering display for me. I knew that I might have reached the point of no return when I insisted there be no tray service during any of the meals. I made the waitstaff carry everything by hand, and then I announced that there would be no fan-folded napkins at my wedding. They folded the napkins according to the patterns that I had chosen and inserted a flower in each and every one. I never would have humored a bride like me. I ended up enjoying my wedding as much as I enjoy hosting sixty strangers on a Friday night.

On the way home with Chris and Kate (who was terrified that she was encroaching on our married space), I turned to them and said, "You know, I had a lot of fun."

Out of the roar of laughter they said, "When was that?"

"I think that I missed that part."

"Where exactly were you when you were having fun?"

"Was I there?"

"Can we do it all over again?"

Three months later we purchased Metro Bis. It all happened so fast that by the time I realized that being the wife of a chef carried certain unwanted responsibilities, it was far too late. We had been married on May 19 (which I engraved on Chris's band, hoping he would remember) and purchased the restaurant on August 12. While Chris finished work at his last job, I mailed out thank-you cards for our wedding gifts, renegotiated the lease for the building, filled out the paperwork for the liquor license (the money from our wedding just covered the application fee), borrowed furniture from our best man, and tried to get financing. We needed money. A lot more money than we had. Actually we had no money. We didn't even have a savings account. Chris found a consultant through a mutual friend, and I wrote a fifty-page business plan to present to the banks. The consultant spent the majority of the time talking about his kids and overcharging us. I went to twenty-five different banks to ask about small-business loans. Some of them told me that I was out of my mind, others told me that I needed money to get money, everybody else told me that I could try to fill out the application form and send it in. After a lot of begging we got independent investors. We're still paying off that debt. When we got their money, we didn't even own our cars yet, and we had a negative net worth of fifteen thousand. We negotiated with the broker for weeks. The price went up and down. The closing attorneys, one of whom was my dad, started to get into a bidding war. I thought that we would never actually own the restaurant. At the closing we signed and signed and signed some more. We owed money to the previous owners (we signed a personal guarantee) and we owed money to the broker who had lent us his fee just to close the sale. At this point we had interviewed all of the waitstaff. Hours after the closing the locks were changed and I went in search of insurance. It occurred to me that someone might hurt themselves while painting. I had scheduled to have the floor redone. My sister and I carried each and every one of the seventy-five marble-topped tables to the office. I couldn't lift my arms for a week. Chris was in the process of painting all of the chairs and framing the mirrors. My parents helped paint the entire inside of the restaurant, and my mother stenciled the bathroom. I lay on the floor in the staggering heat (we couldn't afford to turn on the air-conditioning yet) and just stared at the ceiling. Al, our first sous-chef, painted the ceiling in the kitchen.

The fire inspector came. The health inspector came. We needed a computer. We borrowed another five thousand dollars. The floor refinishers didn't show up. We called. They came the next day. The computer was two days late. Everyone trained on it during our first lunch. Where was the temporary liquor license? I drove into Hartford, waited in line for two hours, and found out that it was in the wrong pile. They asked to see my ID because they didn't think that I was old enough to apply for the permit. I had put it in Chris's name anyway, because I was just going to help out for the first few months, just until everything was running smoothly. I was supposed to discover and follow my own career dreams after I finished working in the restaurant. Then I wrote the employee handbook and typed all of the menus. Eventually the doors opened, and there was a whole new set of problems. There was payroll and security deposits and QuickBooks. QuickBooks, that easy-to-use accounting program. It probably would have been easier if I had taken one accounting class in college, but I hated math. The accountant "trained" me to enter the information in the program, and I thought that I was doing it right until I got my first bank statement. Short of an intercession from above, there was absolutely no way I was going to be able to reconcile those six pieces of paper. During the first week of business we'd charged 8 percent sales tax instead of 6 percent because we had bought the computer from a dealer in New York instead of Connecticut. A very helpful math teacher pointed out our error on a check one Friday during lunch. The bank statement was a mess. American Express, Visa/MasterCard, and cash all entered the account at different times in different amounts.

I was on the floor for lunch and dinner six days a week. We drove in our separate cars for forty-five minutes to get home every night. Sometimes I would fall asleep for a second or two at the wheel before jolting back awake. In the beginning the bills would come in with the drivers in the middle of lunch, and I would have to stop what I was doing, run down to the office, and write a check. Then came all of the credit applications. Every day I filled out five credit applications so that I wouldn't have to run and write checks in the middle of lunch. Eventually we got credit terms, and

I had to set aside time to pay the bills. Tons of bills. Really confusing bills. It seemed as if Chris had a different pur- veyor for every ingredient that he used. To complicate my paperwork further, he sent back at least two items on each invoice because the products weren't up to his standards. I spent my lunch waiting on tables, my afternoons banging my head on my desk until I drew blood, and my evenings waiting on tables. I began an advertising campaign, design- ing the ads myself. I started entering our mailing list on our computer and printed four hundred double-sided sheets of our *Metro Mail* newsletter in batches of twenty-five because the printer would clog otherwise. I designed and printed business cards, pamphlets, and menus.

Then Jerry, our general manager, went back to North Carolina to be with his wife and kids. I didn't know if he was coming back. He had planned on working with us until he had enough money to move them, but it was taking too long and his wife wasn't sure if she wanted to come back to Connecticut. Feeling a little overwhelmed, one day I cried at my desk just prior to lunch service, which made him really uncomfortable. Then I felt bad about crying because I knew he needed to be with his wife and kids. I just didn't think that I could do it on my own. I had so many new responsibilities. I could hardly handle my own work, and I had no idea what he did. We didn't even have anyone working lunch the day he left. It was just me. Jerry came back three weeks later. We had somehow found the money to pay for his moving expenses.

While he was gone I attempted to put through the alcohol order, a process that still remains a mystery to me. A magazine called the *Beverage Journal* arrives by mail once a month. It contains the prices of the liquors that are set by each of the distributors after they are taxed by the state of Connecticut; there is also the suggested retail price for liquor stores, and boxed specials called posts. Some types of alcohol are sold by two distributors, so they have a gentleman's agreement to sell it at the same price. Other brands are exclusively carried by one distributor. These wholesalers have divided the state of Connecticut diagonally in half to form two territories. A handful of distributors compete for business on each side of the state. The *Beverage Journal* includes the price listing for all of the distributors, including those that won't sell to us because we aren't in their territory. Jerry had developed an interesting wine list with wines and beers from six companies in our area. The index of the *Beverage Journal* would have been easy for me to read if I knew what kind of liquor Jack Daniel's was. After I finally went to the bar and discovered that it was a whiskey, I then needed to determine whether it was imported and, most important, which company I needed to order it from. I think that I called Jerry twice a day while he was gone just to get through the ordering and to see if he had convinced his wife that it was a good idea to move back to Connecticut. While he was gone I proved myself to the waitstaff, who had felt that Jerry was the one who was really in charge. I also learned how to make a few of the core drinks, like martinis, Gibsons, and Old-Fashioneds.

One Saturday night as I hosted, bused tables, and ran food, a man approached the bartender and started yelling at her. He had been waiting for twenty minutes for his appetizers, and the tables around him that had sat after he had were already enjoying their food. I ran back to the kitchen to find out where his food was. There was no order. I ran to the computer. There was no order. I attacked the waitress and asked where the order was. She said that the kitchen just didn't have her food yet. I showed her the blank check in the computer; she reached in her pocket and pulled out the carefully transcribed order. I ran back to the kitchen and they dropped everything to get the appetizers to the table right away. I delivered them to the table and explained to the man what had happened to his order. He told me the kitchen was unprepared and that it was completely wrong of me to try to blame the entire situation on the waitress. As they finished their appetizers, I was called to table seven. Their duck had been overcooked as the kitchen scrambled to produce the late appetizers. I went back to the kitchen with the duck and announced that I needed a steak instead. Medium. Now. I switched the waitress to a different table because she refused to go back. The man called me back to the table after he had eaten two bites of his Caesar salad.

"Cancel my order," he demanded. "I've waited too long, and I'm not hungry anymore."

I politely inquired whether everyone at the table wanted their orders canceled. Nope. Just him. The entrées came out fast while he sat with an empty space in front of him. He asked for the bill. The waitress told him that there would be no bill, and he rose abruptly from the table. He walked out the front door with his wife rushing behind, and the extremely quiet couple who had joined him followed after leaving sixty dollars on the table. The first waitress—the one who had forgotten to put the order in the computer—picked up the "tip" while I cleared the table. I was just glad that the guy didn't firebomb the bar on his way out. We hadn't paid for it yet.

It was during this same painful week that I was first shackled by my role as the wife of the chef. There were three older women at table four during a September lunch. They were asking questions about the new ownership and I told them that my husband (the chef) and I owned the restaurant. One woman turned to the other and said, "Isn't this nice, she's the wife of the chef."

When I actually had the gall to insist that I, too, owned the restaurant, they smiled at me with the oh-yes-honey-we-understand smile.

PUTTING AWAY
THE PICKLES

*L*unch today is a madhouse. The waitstaff sat the entire room at once. The sound of fifty people making business deals and opening birthday presents is deafening in the small room. I had entered through the back door of the kitchen. On my way past the line I picked up the food for table seven. The woman is out of iced tea, so I refill her glass. Then I take a run through the dining room with the water pitcher. It's like a desert out here. Tables three, ten, and fifteen need bread. Six, five, and nineteen need to be cleared. I cut three baskets of bread, fill three ramekins with hummus. The waiter takes them from me, so I fill a bowl of soup for table nine. Soup and salad reach the table. I clear table six because it's next to nine. They want to wrap half of their turkey sandwich, and they need the check. I head for the kitchen, stop at the line, and place the sandwich in a takeout container. Jerry rushes by with two handfuls of glasses.

"Table four wants to talk to you about food for a party this weekend," he says as he drops the glasses in the rack.

"Can you run this sandwich to position two on six? And

drop a check," I reply. Jerry takes the sandwich wrapped to go.

"Someone from the bank has called three times this morning," he says on his way out of the kitchen. A half second passes while I think about which tables I was going to clear.

Chris says, "Make these desserts. We're in the weeds." I grab the ticket that he just handed me and slide around the corner to the dessert station. Apple tart, chocolate tart, key lime tart. I reach in the fridge, grab an apple tart, toss it on a sizzle platter, and send it down the table to the oven. Chris pops it in the oven while I pull two plates and decorate them for the chocolate tart and key lime. I push a key lime tart from the sheet pan in the fridge onto its plate. Whip cream, add berries, mint, a decorative cookie, a dusting of cinnamon, and I push the plate to the front of the table.

"Pull my apple tart," I tell Chris as I force the too-cold chocolate sauce out of the bottle and onto the plate.

He slides the tart back down the table. I reach in the fridge for a chocolate tart and place it in the center of my plate. I can hear the apple tart sizzling to my right as I grab the blowtorch. I put the flame to the chocolate for two seconds to take the chill off. Whip cream, add berries, mint, decorative cookie, chocolate dust, to the front of the table. I grab another plate and ladle on warm caramel sauce for the apple tart.

I can hear the phone ringing in the dining room; no one is answering it, so I drop what I'm doing.

"Good afternoon, Metro Bis," I yell over the din of the dining room.

"Hello? Is this Metro Bis?"

"Yes it is. How can I help you?"

"I was wondering what kind of things you have on your lunch menu."

"We have sandwiches, salads, pastas, and some heartier entrées."

"What kind of sandwiches do you have?"

"Hold on just one moment, ma'am," I sigh as I head for the hostess stand and the menus. "Hello, I have a portobello sandwich with grilled portobello mushroom on a toasted baguette with slow-roasted tomatoes, fresh mozzarella, and tomato aioli. I have a smoked turkey breast on toasted marble rye bread with roasted pepper salad and Brie cheese. Could you hold for just one moment, please?"

Two people have just walked in the door, and the other line is ringing. I answer the other line first.

"Good afternoon, Metro Bis."

"Hello, may I please speak with the owner?"

"I'm sorry, she's not available right now," I lied. "May I take a message?"

"This is Mary calling from AT&T Internet services. Do you have a computer with Internet access?"

"I'm sorry, you've called a restaurant in the middle of lunch service. I don't have time to talk to you right now. Good-bye."

Jerry seats the two people at the door, and I pick up line one again.

"Hello?"

"Yes, I'm still here."

"Okay, we also have a steak sandwich and a chicken sandwich."

"What is the steak sandwich served with?"

"Caramelized onions and Asian slaw."

"What's Asian slaw?"

"It's kind of like coleslaw, but it has Asian spices."

"I don't know if I'd like that."

"Uh-huh."

"How much was the portobello mushroom sandwich?"

"Seven ninety-five."

"Is that good?"

"Yes."

"Okay, I'd like to make a reservation for next Wednesday lunch at twelve for two people."

I rush back through the dining room to check on the desserts. On my way through I clear table fifteen. Table sixteen asks for some butter. I drop my plates on the pile in the dishwashing section and go back to the desserts. Chris didn't get a chance to finish them for me. I bend over and stretch into the freezer. I use a bowl perched on top of the vanilla and pop open the three gallon buckets until I find the sorbet. Three sorbet balls in the bowl. I switch scoops so I have a hot one, pull out a ball of vanilla, and place it on top of the apple tart. I open the dessert fridge one last time and push everything back in, take a plate out, find a doily, put the bowl of sorbet on the plate, pick up the rest of the desserts, and go to table seventeen. Six has left, so I clear their coffee cups and water glasses. Jerry swings by on his way to the kitchen with the plates from twelve.

"Can you get the delivery at the door?" he asks. "Did you make it to four yet?"

"I'm sorry. I just had one of those lonely-people calls."

"Ugh. Those are the worst. Did she make you read the whole menu?"

"Just about. I got the door."

I head back to the kitchen with the contents of table six. The dishwashing station is overrun with dishes. I take a couple of seconds to stack the dishes so they don't fall on the floor, wash my hands, walk the length of the dining room, and greet the UPS guy. It's the kids' meal bags I ordered COD. I tear the invoice off the box, run to the office for a check, race back upstairs, and sign for the package. Then I find a piece of paper and a pen and head to table four.

"Jerry said that you're interested in food for this upcoming weekend."

"Oh yes, we're having twelve people over for a shower."

"Have you seen our catering menu?"

"No, do you have one?" I head to the hostess stand for a catering menu. There are none. I walk back to the office, get a menu, and go back to four.

"Oh wow, look at this menu. I have no idea what I want. Can I take this home, look it over, and give you a call back?"

"Sure. Have a great afternoon." As I walk back to the kitchen, I'm told that we've eighty-sixed the chicken sandwich.

"Excuse me, can you tell me where the bathroom is?"

"Head toward the kitchen and take a right." I clear and reset four tables, pour two glasses of white wine, take a tea to position three on twenty, and make a break for the office.

On my way through the kitchen Chris stops me. "Cynthia called. She wants the descriptions for the dinners we donated for the auction this Sunday."

"I'll e-mail her this afternoon. Did you make lasagne for Express yet?"

"I'm working on it." I pass the dishwasher repairman on my way out the back door.

2

AFTERNOON

PULLING OUT
THE KNIVES

$\mathcal{F}$inally my desk. I sink into my chair. What was I supposed to do today? Sometimes I think that it would be easier to work in the kitchen, especially in the afternoon. You could be totally hung over with two hours of sleep, step into the walk-in, and realize that you needed to make whipped potatoes. Everything has a priority. It's not that easy, of course; Chris has a page-long prep sheet every day from which he assigns each task to a different member of the kitchen based on his or her skill level. The afternoon is filled with cooking, slicing, roasting, picking, chopping, and organizing for dinner service. I look at my calendar. I have a four o'clock appointment with an advertising salesman. That gives me enough time to enter sales on the computer, call the accountant, and run to the bank. Just as I open my desk drawer to take out my staple remover, calculator, and pencil, the intercom rings from upstairs.

"There's someone here about a job. Can you talk to him?" Chris asks.

"What position?"

"Line cook."

"Why do you want me to talk to him?"

"Just take his information and see if you think I should meet with him."

Just as I'm about to argue, I hear a knock at the office door.

"Come in," I say as I hang up on Chris.

I'm obviously going to be meeting with this guy whether I want to or not. He's in his early twenties and is very well dressed. Too well dressed for a kitchen job. He has on a suit and tie, and I now know why they sent him to me. I shake his hand and he takes a seat. He hands me a résumé and tells me what job he wants. He doesn't tell me why he wants to work for Metro Bis, which is his first mistake. His second mistake is handing me his résumé. As he's talking I'm reading it, and I almost explode with laughter. Under the description of his last job it says, "Worked at X restaurant, the best restaurant in the state of Connecticut." I can't resist.

"Why did you leave the best restaurant in the state of Connecticut?"

"The chef was a jerk."

Strike three. Get out. I tell him that I'll give Chris his résumé. I'm not sure if we are even hiring. After he leaves I put his paperwork in my application file. I doubt that Chris will even ask me about him.

Back to my sales. I take for granted how quickly I can enter sales now in the computer, and do payroll, file taxes, and organize the bills. It wasn't always so easy.

MONEY, MONEY, MONEY

In Austria all business own- ers must attend school for two years before they can set up shop. What a novel idea. There are so many things I wish I had learned ahead of time. My first business headache started with my accounting firm. Even though they did my payroll well, they didn't teach me how to enter sales in the computer properly, and I couldn't balance my bank statements. So I found a new accountant and had to find another company to do payroll. I switched to the largest payroll-processing company in the country and was fine until three months later when they lost the payroll worksheet that I faxed to them and sent my tax payments out a month late. I was told I would incur tax penalties as a result. I abruptly switched to a really, really small company that was just getting started. I explained that I wanted the entire payroll with paychecks and taxes to come from my bank account in one lump sum because it is easier for me to track on my statement. The full amount would be deposited in the payroll company's account, and they would write the paychecks from their account. None of this happened. The taxes didn't come out and all of the employee paychecks came out separately from my account. When I spoke with the payroll company, the salesman was rude and insisted that we had agreed that payroll would be done in this manner. I decided to switch to another company after I discovered he was a business partner in a local restaurant. It doesn't take a genius to make a rough estimate of our sales based on the waitstaff's tip claims. When I finally switched payroll companies, the salesman billed me for a three-hundred-dollar setup fee, which was never discussed. When I didn't pay he removed his fee from my bank account. I had given the company permission to remove payroll and taxes from my account, not the fee. I went to the police, and the company finally decided to return my money.

Just as I was settling into the third payroll company, I learned an odd lesson about unemployment insurance, that percentage of payroll that all employers pay to offset the expense of unemployment claims. In the state of Connecticut a business can take over an existing business's unemployment insurance rate during the sale if the new owner retains most of the assets and employees. The starting rate for new businesses when we took over was 3.5 percent (it's now down to 2.9 percent). If you have many unemployment claims, then you max out at 5.4 percent; if you don't have any, then you pay the minimum of 0.5 percent. The previous owners had a rate of 2.5 percent. When a business takes over an unemployment insurance rate, the buyer also takes on any of the previous employees' unemployment claims. We hired most of the workers from the last ownership for the first few months we were open until they moved on. There were only three who didn't work with us. One was a pastry chef whom we could have used, but she was loyal to the previous owners. Another was a college student who was working only the summer season and didn't care about new employers. The third was the chef. He was apparently quite a tyrant. The waitstaff were frightened by his skinhead and tattooed appearance. The owners must have been frightened, too, because they paid him twenty-four dollars an hour. He was angry whenever the floor staff sat diners without reservations, and he closed after the last reservation came in. This was a problem if the last reservation was at seven-thirty. But this is all rumor. I never actually met with him. He avoided us as we interviewed the staff. We could have used him in the kitchen, but he wouldn't talk to Chris. Soon the new Metro Bis was up and running, and I forgot about him until I got a statement from the Department of Labor requesting fifteen hundred dollars and a court appearance.

Stressed to the point of nausea, I drove up to the unemployment building for the hearing. The mediator asked me questions, asked the ex-chef questions, and then I went back to work. The decision came back in my favor, and so far I've avoided another unemployment hearing. Knock on wood. Big wood. Like a two-hundred-year-old redwood. It's just a matter of time before I go back, but I'll at least know the reason why next time.

I just received a nice, fat bill from the Bureau of Alcohol, Tobacco, and Firearms. It seems as though I was supposed to pay an alcohol-selling tax. I had no idea that restaurants were regulated by the ATF; I thought they just wandered around the country looking for crazy men whose cabins are filled with artillery. There was a penalty for not filing, plus interest that needed to be paid on three years of tax; I figure that I could have saved myself at least a couple hundred dollars had I known what I was doing.

I also learned a lot more about the health department regulations. Chris was already familiar with their role, having dealt with health inspectors at all of the other restaurants where he had been employed. The inspector usually comes in the morning with a checklist of guidelines that we are supposed to follow. The list includes things like providing paper towels for your employees to dry their hands, making sure your refrigerator temperatures are between 33 and 45 degrees, and having a clean working environment. Most of the guidelines are assigned a value of 1 to 2 points; any that are not followed are subtracted from the perfect score of 100. There are a few 4-point violations such as getting your meat from a hunter down the street rather than from a USDA-regulated processing center, storing toxic cleaning solutions in your prep area instead of by the dishwasher, and allowing your raw chicken to drip onto your fresh vegetables in the walk-in rather than separating these products and storing them properly. Four-point violations are taken very seriously by the health department because they may create a risk to the public. Any score below 70 results in a warning and another inspection thirty days later.

Health regulations are very important, but not all restaurants are examined equally. All inspectors interpret the guidelines as they see fit, and they each have their own pet peeves. Some inspectors are biased against certain ethnic restaurants because they don't feel that these groups maintain proper health standards. We've had inspectors who take points off because the refrigerator seals need to be replaced, because tongs are hanging on the oven door handles, because the scoop was left in the flour. Another inspector might overlook these violations and focus on the cleanliness of the soda gun or the ceiling vents. No restaurant ever gets a perfect score because there is always something that needs to be improved.

The health department in our area has recently enacted two new regulations. Our menu now carries a warning, "Thoroughly cooking meats, poultry, seafood, shellfish, or eggs reduces the risk of food borne illness," and we are required to post a piece of paper with little waiters on it in our entryway. The number of waiters that the restaurant receives is supposed to indicate cleanliness to the dining public. Three waiters is the best and no waiters is the worst. This paper is deceiving, though, because the number of waiters a restaurant is given is not based on the restaurant's health score. It is left to the inspector to decide how many waiters to give. Our current inspector bases his decision on his overall impression of cleanliness. Our last inspector chose the number of waiters depending on how much the restaurant improved from one inspection to the next.

These little waiters aren't that bad, though. In the state of North Carolina and the counties of San Diego and Los Angeles the restaurants are required to post the results of their most recent health inspection as a letter grade on their front door. In North Carolina most of the restaurants receive an A marking. In Dallas, Seattle, Denver, and New York City the results of all inspections are now available on-line. The public everywhere has access to every restaurant's health report by stopping by the local department. I believe customers should have a right to examine these reports, but they should also know why these restaurants received their markings. Le Bernardin, a prominent New York City restaurant, had a vermin violation on their report right after New York went on-line. They were very upset that this information was made public because mouse droppings had been discovered on a product they were sending back. The vermin weren't present in the restaurant; they were living at the distributor. The health department is in place to protect the public, not to cause mass hysteria. It is important for people to have all of the available information rather than just a B or a 72.

But the aspect of business that I wish I knew the most about is immigration law. I am proud to say that we are probably one of the few restaurants in the country that doesn't hire illegal immigrants without paperwork. At least not knowingly. The I-9 proof-of-work-eligibility form is useless. Social Security cards, driver's licenses, even passports can all be had for a price. Here's the part that bothers me. A woman comes to the United States from Mexico, Jamaica, Ecuador, or some other place on some sort of work visa. She is willing to work hard. She cleans bathrooms, mops floors, washes dishes. She shows up for work every day on time, she doesn't have an attitude, she takes night classes to learn more English, and she keeps to herself. She wants to be a legal citizen, but she has no skills and no family living in the United States, so she can't get a green card. She goes back to her country when her work visa runs out, and she spends the next six months trying to get back because she wants to be legal.

Some people want to keep the United States for the Americans, but they have forgotten how their families arrived in this country. They feel that immigrants are stealing jobs from Americans, but most established citizens don't want to fill restaurant positions. We are almost constantly searching for dishwashers. The average turnover in restaurants with a check average over fifteen dollars per person is 76 percent a year. I've had fifty-eight employees to fill twelve positions in two years, four months, and seven days. Open every single restaurant trade magazine published in the past year and every issue has a new take on the "labor crisis." The National Restaurant Association is lobbying to open the borders and fill more positions. With 11.3 million employees, the restaurant business is the second largest employer in the country next to the government, and we can feel the labor shortage in Simsbury, Connecticut. McDonald's, on the other side of town, has a starting rate of eight dollars per hour with benefits. The entire American economy would collapse if not for the work of illegal immigrants. Ever been to Dallas during the summer? Ever wonder why Dallas is one of the fastest-growing cities in the United States? Yes, money, but who is working construction, installing pools, paving parking lots? Thousands of immigrants. But this is another story. For me it's not about the legal issues of immigration. It's about having a reliable dishwasher on Saturday night.

Restaurant employment problems don't end there. I won't easily forget the day I opened the letter from the Federal Department of Labor and found that I was the target of an audit for no reason. Just random. They had decided to see if the labor laws were being followed in a handful of Connecticut restaurants. We don't have many workers under the age of eighteen, so we weren't in violation of child labor laws, but we did learn a lesson about salaried employees. We have only two employees on salary, our sous-chef and our general manager. Everyone else is paid by the hour. We've worked in places where the dishwashers were paid on salary—but they worked eighty hours a week, which averaged to about $2.50 an hour. Our two salaried employees work fifty hours a week. The woman from the labor board had no problem with our general manager being on salary. Her problem was with our sous-chef. According to law, he wasn't allowed to be on salary because he performs manual labor. Well, Chris performs manual labor, too. What's the big deal? The auditor finally let us off the hook when she realized that our sous-chef position included enough managerial responsibilities like ordering and overseeing the staff in addition to the manual labor. The National Restaurant Association is attempting to change this law, too. I hope that they can find a way to protect the eighty-hour-a-week dishwasher and help legitimate business owners provide a reliable, fixed income to their top managerial staff on salary.

The restaurant business employs more ex–welfare recipients, ex–disabled people, and ex-cons than any other. Our business is about second chances and first chances. We employ the most teenagers and offer the most upward mobility for anyone from anywhere who is willing to work hard. There are so many stories of young people successful in management positions. The founders of Subway were eighteen when they started their business in Connecticut. There are countless chefs who started as dishwashers and worked their way through the ranks of the kitchen.

Chris and I struggle, and we always lie about it. We lived off of our credit cards for almost two years. We're in debt up to our eyebrows, but you would hardly know it by talking to us. Chris says that you can smell the death of a restaurant way before it happens. "Always tell everyone that you're doing really well, that you're really busy," he says emphatically. The restaurant does really well. We always pay all of our bills, and we've never bounced payroll, as some restaurants have been known to do. Chris and I do okay. Our sous-chef and our manager make more money than the two of us, and our full-time waiters claim more in tips each year than we take home. But we've stopped having to use our credit cards to buy shampoo and toothpaste. Now we're just in debt. We've increased our sales, but we increased payroll, too. Then sales dropped and payroll was too high. All of the extra money goes to the debt. Most high-end restaurants make only 5 to 12 percent profit. Forty percent of the profit goes to our investors. Thank God for the power of plastic. Seven dollars for a glass of wine might seem like a lot, but profits are very low.

We've lived in the same apartment for two years. Whenever there is a holiday or a birthday, I always ask my parents for things I need like a vacuum cleaner, curtains, or a rug. During the first year we owned Metro Bis I gave Chris three pairs of underwear and fifteen boxes of frozen peas for Christmas. It is strange to work seventy hours a week and not make any money. We personally have no money saved. I lost my health insurance from my father's COBRA plan after I graduated from college. I would like to have insurance, and I would like my employees to have insurance, too.

I often ask new employees what they would do if they had a million dollars. I've had many responses, including go back to Mexico, travel around the world, buy a car, save some for retirement, and give the rest to their parents. I would pay off the debt. I picture the debt as a huge red ball, like the kind that you might find in a gymnasium. It's so big that it should crush me, but it is so light that I'm just stuck awkwardly roaming around with it. I'm not overly materialistic and don't require much to live on, but I would like to burst the debt, buy a new computer, improve the restaurant, offer insurance, save for retirement, and so on. I often wish that I could talk about the financial sacrifices that all business owners make, but people would think that the restaurant isn't doing well. We make those choices so that the restaurant will flourish and our employees are happy. It would be nice if Chris and I had a regular paycheck and could save money for a home, but that won't happen for a long, long time.

I'm not so sure that I want a home, anyway. I would be the one on the lawn mower with a flashlight at ten o'clock on a Tuesday night. I would be the one shoveling the driveway and raking the leaves, and Chris would be the one entertaining. I wouldn't mind the company as much as I would mind inviting people over to worship him. Whenever Chris is in a domestic kitchen, people crowd around him and admire his techniques. They admire his knife skills and try to get close enough to learn a secret that they can pretend is all theirs. Most of the time it makes me irritated, or I just want to vomit. He gets all of the attention and all of the credit all of the time, and I'm left by myself, a pouting child. Nothing that I do brings sighs of joy or deep admiration. No one flocks to me when I write checks. Occasionally someone lets me know that "behind every successful man is a successful woman," or that I must be the organized one because he's so creative. All of my so-called compliments are phrased as insults. Everything that I do is in comparison to him. A chef doesn't just cook and people come. While he may have flashier skills, my abilities make his creativity possible.

But his creativity is also influenced by our need to survive financially. When Chris worked at Mark's Place in Miami, it was one of the top restaurants in the country. He calls it the French Laundry of its day (in other words, a destination restaurant). The chef/owner, Mark Militello, was constantly on the move and promoting his restaurant through charity functions. Chris met Emeril Lagasse before he became *Emeril* and Todd English before he was dubbed "the Wolfgang Puck of the East Coast." When Todd arrived for his charity function at Mark's, the multitude of line cooks perused his menus on display in the entryway. They were shocked and amused as they read his appetizers and entrées.

Apparently his Olives restaurant in Boston was serving pizza and pasta. Todd's charity menu was full of foie gras and caviar. At the end of the evening, after an impressive meal, Chris asked Todd why he was serving pasta and pizza when he was clearly capable of much more refined and intricate cooking. Todd smirked and said, "First you have to give them what they want. Then you can give them what *you* want."

Chris isn't the kind of guy who remembers much, but this comment stuck with him, especially during our first few months at Metro Bis. Dishes that had sold by the hundreds at the last restaurant he worked for in New Milford weren't even ordered in Simsbury. He tried to sell a fresh calamari steak, but the customers poked at it and sent it back. He tried the fried popcorn shrimp appetizer that he'd sold by the gallon, but no one ordered it. Eventually, after much anguish and subsequent blows to the ego, Chris introduced crab cakes. They are still on the menu, and we sell close to one hundred orders a week. The crab cakes are rich, delicate patties made from crab meat with just a little bit of stuffing, and they bore Chris to tears. He just wants to take them off the menu, but he can't. It's what the customers want, and we haven't yet reached the point where we can make what we want (except for New Year's Eve and wine dinners). To keep Chris's spirits up, we have also introduced a private tasting menu. Parties of six can order this dinner paired with Robert Mondavi wines. Finally, Chris can cook what he wants.

There are many balancing acts in this business. You need to make money, but you want to create a great product. You want to cook what you love, but not everyone has the same tastes that you do. One weekend a younger couple walked in, looked at the menu, smiled, and said, "Thanks, but I think this is a little too foo-foo for us." Okay. I offered our steak, which can be ordered without the Gorgonzola cheese on top, or a plain pasta, but they just shook their heads. I wished them a good evening and glanced back at the kitchen. Chris was smiling at me from across the dining room filled with the adventurous souls who ordered raw tuna and other strange "foo-foo" items from the menu. Each day gets better: There are more people who want to try something different. But there are also those diners who want familiar foods that they feel comfortable with. So we have some of both, and we stay in business.

The restaurant industry is unbelievably competitive. Only one half of all restaurants opened this year will be open a year from now. Only one in ten will make it to five years. (This is one of the main reasons I couldn't get a bank loan.) But it's not just about competing for customers. Chefs compete with one another. They steal recipes, ideas, wives, equipment, and employees. It is not uncommon for a member of the waitstaff to receive a business card from a chef in the area "just in case" they need another job. When attending a charity event, chefs stroll from one food display to another, glancing down their noses to assess the presentation, food combinations, and finally (if they dare) the taste of an item. Chefs compete for airtime, newspaper articles, and the spotlight. They try to get the best ingredients and the best wine.

Most of the high-end wines are allocated. There might be only two cases of Harlan, Dominus, Screaming Eagle, or specialty French Bordeauxs and Burgundies that come to Connecticut in a given year. Every chef, general manager, and owner wants that wine and will try to get it, but only the restaurants that have high-volume alcohol sales or statewide reputations, or know someone at the top of the vineyard or distributor, will even know about it. Everyone else will be told that the casinos got it or it just didn't come in. Some vineyards, like Silver Oaks, decide that their wines should be sold only in restaurants. Salesmen who want to earn more business from liquor stores will try to run a paper trail for the wine through our restaurant and sell it to the package store down the street. Once Jerry sees a wine that is allocated for restaurants in a store, he refuses to carry it out of principle.

The wine business is also known for its "gray market," the term that refers to when alcohol that is supposed to be regulated by each state wanders over borders tax free. In a high-volume restaurant the wine salesman will try to sell twenty-five cases of something that isn't moving off the warehouse floor. He'll offer the restaurant a buy-four-get-one-free deal to move the merchandise. The fifth case is unregulated by the state and will show up in the salesman's car after the rest of the delivery. Connecticut is one of the stricter states for alcohol regulation, so the gray market isn't as accessible to restaurants. Each state has its own regulations, like South Carolina, where all liquors and wines are stored in the tiny bottles that airlines serve. In Massachusetts the price of alcohol works on more of a haggling system. There is a printed price booklet like there is in Connecticut, but the prices are negotiable. The standard markup for alcohol nationwide is 25 to 30 percent for retail and 150 percent for restaurants. We charge a markup of 100 percent on most items because we want to be fair and would like the diners to enjoy wine with their meals. Plus, reasonable bottle prices encourage diners to buy more.

Food works on a bargaining system, too, and there are many unwritten rules. Ever since someone was shot in front of the factory one morning, I've always made sure to pay the bread company on time. There are rumors that the mob controls portions of the food supply, linen companies, and garbage removal services. I don't want to find out if the rumors are true.

We were out of calamari once for a week while our fish company tried to find a new brand. The calamari was no longer allowed to be imported after the United States government found some sort of illegal substance packed with it. We never did find out what it was, and I'm sure it's better we not know. I'm never late on my caviar payment, either, because those fish eggs have been known to slip into the country when no one's looking. The illegal market for caviar is a problem that has led to worldwide smuggling.

For these reasons and more, including weather and war, purveyors have a range of quality among their products, especially produce. Prices and quality are haggled over every day. Chris spent an entire six hours one day screaming at the produce company after returning from a charity event. Apparently the chef on the table next to him received microgreens (really small herb shoots) on the same day Chris did, from the same company, but whereas this chef got the good greens, Chris received the ones that had been sitting in the warehouse for the past week. I don't know too much about distribution, but I figure some guy just putters around in the biggest refrigerator in the world gathering the ingredients for each order. I don't think that this guy cares too much about quality, he's just getting everything ready for the trucks. Chris tells me that the salesman will actually select the items personally from the warehouse if the guy gathering for the trucks keeps on sending you crap. (He must be right because he got me the world's largest watermelon for my birthday one year. He asked his saleswoman to hand-pick the biggest melon she could find, and I wasn't disappointed. It weighed no less than fifty pounds, and Chris had a hard time getting it into the house. We took out all the shelves from our fridge, and we still had to cut it in half.) The point wasn't so much that Chris's product was mediocre (a lot of produce isn't that beautiful after traveling thousands of miles); it was that the other chef got the better microgreens, which made Chris look bad. The produce company couldn't tell him that the greens were just low quality this week because Chris had proof that that wasn't the case. He had seen the good ones, and he was tormented. Chefs have to keep struggling for the best products, the best dishes, and the best staff because restaurants that aren't working hard to be better every day are the ones that are closed the next year.

This inevitable sense of doom and the constant feeling that you are trying to outrun Satan force me to be more creative. I have to set our restaurant apart. I have to make sure that every potential customer knows who we are and what makes us different. My most recent project was the bottling of Chris's salad dressings. We use these every day in the restaurant, and they are so popular that we decided to sell them. It took me almost a year and a half to complete this project. I spent months searching for the right bottle. It couldn't be too expensive, the kitchen staff had to like it, and it had to be the right size. Then the label had to be designed. A closure for the bottle, a bar code, exemption from FDA labeling requirements, pestering the food scientist to determine if the pH is low enough. Chris needed to decide whether a stabilizer was necessary and if organic ketchup should be ordered to retain the all-natural statement on the label. He changed the order of the ingredients on each label twice and complained about the color of the tomato in one of the prototype drawings. I named the dressings Prosperi of Metro Bis so that we could carry the name over to other products like BBQ sauce or Thai dressings. Customers sometimes ask which company packs the dressing for us, assuming that I no longer have anything to do with it.

The salad dressing is a huge pain in the ass, but I love it. First the bottles must be heated to 75 degrees in the microwave so that the label will stick. I lay the warm bottles on their sides, center the labels as well as possible, then wrap them around each side. Then the bottles must be left in a warm environment for an hour so the labels can continue to adhere. Next the dressing comes down from the kitchen in five-gallon buckets. I grab a funnel and get to work. After each bottle is filled and I can't stand the smell of Caesar any longer, I moisten the cork with some dressing. This helps to push it into the bottle. Next the foil goes on like it does on a wine bottle. I get the heat sealer we call "the hair dryer from hell" (it would burn the hair right off your head) from storage. I turn it on, wait till it's really hot, then heat-seal each foil. Next the date is stamped by hand above the bar code, and the whole package goes in the fridge. It's so easy. I just don't understand why my employees in Metro Express want me dead.

I have now passed on most of the bottling work to them.

One of the first times I was packing dressing in a crunch, I asked Chris what it was like to have his name on a product. He looked puzzled.

"I haven't had any time to think about it," he said. "How much more salad dressing do you need?"

Maybe if he stared at the Prosperi label for three hours, he'd feel differently about it.

THERE IS NO salad dressing that I need to help pack today. Instead I'm in the office banging numbers into the keyboard, getting the bank deposit ready, arguing on the phone with the produce company about an unpaid invoice, calling the accountant about my property taxes, and then I leave for the bank and the post office. While I'm out I run into the pharmacy to grab my prescription. In the doorway I greet a customer.

"Taking the day off, I see," she says, smirking.

"No, Ms. Fletcher. It's in between lunch and dinner. I'm running my errands."

"Humph," she replies.

I make my way to the prescription counter and talk to the pharmacist, whose stepson used to work in the kitchen. My drugs aren't ready yet, so I sit in the waiting area. The woman on my left turns to me.

"What's the soup today, dearie?"

"Oh, hello, Ms. Mitchell. I didn't see you there. I think

that the soups today are butternut squash and cider bisque and potato leek and Cheddar."

"Oh, that's too bad. I really wanted to have a cup of that Asian beef stew."

As the conversation trails off with obvious disappointment, I feel a small tap on my knee and look to my right. A beaming three-year-old Victoria is staring at me.

"How are you today?" I ask. She just keeps on smiling and staring.

Her mother smiles at me, too, and says to her daughter, "Do you know who that is, honey? It's the macaroni-and-cheese lady."

I smile, wave, grab my prescription, and run for the door. One more stop at the hardware store to make some extra keys, and I make it back in time for my four o'clock appointment. The phone rings just as the salesman is coming through the door. The March of Dimes wants to know what Chris will be serving at their fund-raiser next week. I intercom upstairs. No one knows where he went. I tell the March of Dimes that he'll probably serve corn cakes with smoked salmon and that I'll check with him and call back later. The salesman settles in with his laptop computer and all of his paperwork.

"This is our magazine," he tells me. "This is our Web site. Special restaurant rate. Look at all the other restaurants participating. Do you want to sign an advertising contract for the year?"

I'm not so sure that I can make a decision right now, so I use my best excuse and tell the guy that I need to talk it over with my husband. This is a load of bull, but it buys me the time I need even if it makes me look like a brainless wife.

"Of course. I'll call next week for your answer," he says.

As he's leaving I remember how I used to meet with anyone when we first bought the business, no matter what they were selling. I figured that I might learn something along the way, and it broke up the demanding schedule of my day. The salesperson was a person who was there to service me. I took a perverse joy in the controlling aspect of the situation. I had the power to say yes or no, which I quickly got over after one particular meeting during the first three months we were in business. The man from the consulting firm walked into my office, where I sat hunched over my desk attempting to solve the mysteries of QuickBooks. He hesitated for a moment, then asked to meet with Courtney.

"That's me," I said.

He looked at me for a second too long, sat down, and began his spiel. Spend no money unless we increase your sales by 10 percent over three months. Then it's just five thousand dollars. He explained that he had operated several restaurants in the past and that he was very good at consulting. As I glanced over his manipulative paperwork, which he had slid across my desk, I felt him staring at me.

"So," he said slowly. "You own the restaurant?" I didn't look up.

"Yup."

"With your family?" he inquired. I raised my eyes with a look that would have killed any reasonably intelligent man who had ever encountered an angry woman during his time on earth.

In my iciest voice, with careful overpronunciation, I said, "What . . . do . . . you . . . mean?"

He briefly faltered. "I mean, uh, do your parents own it? Is it family run?"

I continued my battle and just said, "No." I let the uncomfortable silence linger in the air, felt bad for him, and told him that my husband and I owned the restaurant. I immediately regretted my decision when he sighed with relief, smiled condescendingly, and said, "Ooh. Can I talk to him?"

I don't remember what I did next. I think that I told him that my husband wasn't available. Even though I was somewhat offended, I do remember thinking that it was funny that he wanted to talk to Chris. If you aren't selling food, fixing an appliance, or working in the kitchen, then Chris doesn't have time for you. Chris never would have met with this guy in the first place. He wasn't interested in what anyone had to sell. In fact, Chris would have yelled at the guy for calling in the middle of lunch, hung up on him, and he never would have gotten an appointment. That wasn't such a bad thing. I realized that I shouldn't have met with him, either.

IT'S NOT so bad now. I'm more careful about how I spend my time. As I ponder the huge pile of crap on my desk that floats from one day to the next until it reaches its deadline and is either thrown away or quickly processed, it occurs to me that I haven't eaten anything yet today. Or maybe I did. Did I have a yogurt? I can't remember. I know that I should be sorting through the requests for donations, but I really need to eat something before dinner starts. I head back to the kitchen.

I don't ever work in the kitchen unless we are short-staffed during the holidays. I don't mind doing prep work despite my lack of skill. I make sure I am assigned to tasks that don't include knives. I don't know how to use one despite the numerous lessons I have received. It's better that I don't contribute to the stress of the kitchen. Nothing is more distracting to a chef than watching an inexperienced person attempt to slice a carrot into sticks. So I clean mushrooms, peel potatoes, dice tomatoes (with the vertical dicing machine; no one has lost a finger using it yet), and weigh ingredients. I try not to ask any stupid questions. I once saw a chef go into full meltdown after a line cook asked him twenty-five times which pan should be used for boiling three eggs. Sometimes Chris will have me peel potatoes with the dishwasher to see if he really is way too slow. If the dishwasher beats me, then we know that he must be a good worker. I just try to stay quiet and get my work done as quickly as I can.

It's not a good idea to talk a lot in the kitchen, especially during service. Anything extraneous is left out. Fire fifteen. Pick up six. Ordering baby greens, spinach, and calamari. There is no swearing allowed in our kitchen during service because it is so open to the dining room. We used to have a bank where we had to put dollar bills if we swore, but we haven't had to contribute in a long time. In the afternoon the language is more coarse. Swearing is used in a humorous manner between lunch and dinner, and no one is allowed to curse at anyone else. This type of language makes everyone in the kitchen equal. The chef, the waiter, and the dishwasher are all on the same level when they use the same language. Even if the chef is in charge, the waiter is earning her master's degree in marketing, and the dishwasher just got off the boat from Jamaica. It breaks the social, economic, and racial barriers, allowing everyone to relate to one another and bringing them closer together. I swear when I'm trying to make a connection with an employee and use more formalized language when I'm speaking with authority. Prep time in between lunch and dinner is low stress, so swearing and socializing take place without the pressures of service.

THE RULES
OF THE JUNGLE

In the afternoon the kitchen is in a state of controlled chaos. Crumpled, stained recipes are pulled from a folder, ingredients are carried in and out of the walk-in, and the counter is covered with cutting boards. The slicer, burr mixer (a giant stick with sharp rotating blades at one end), the Robot Coupe (a food processor), and the cheese grater are removed from the shelves and set to work. Scale, mixing bowls, and baking pans are moved methodically from the counter to the dishwasher and back to the counter again. The stove is crowded with pots loaded with sauces, vegetables, and desserts that have to be finished before dinner. Mushrooms are grilled, potato garnishes are fried, and the dense, moist air is filled with the smell of the kitchen. It's my favorite time of the day. There is something magical about the way dishes come together. Throw chicken bones, celery, and carrots in a pot and out comes soup. Combine eggs, cream, and sugar, and crème brûlée is born. Any decent chef always has at least three projects going in the afternoon. While Chris filets and portions salmon, he's roasting parsnips in the oven, simmering his tomato sauce, and waiting for the shrimp to chill in the fridge. Each kitchen employee has a different job to do, and everything comes together just before dinner.

The afternoon prep work always fascinates me, and it's a lot of fun. The chefs are usually relaxed and talkative while they rotate through their duties. At the restaurant where I met Chris it was pretty quiet between lunch and dinner, except for the blaring boom box. Chris and his sous-chef would listen to Live as loud as the volume would go and prep like madmen. They didn't have enough staff to get everything done and had to keep working after service, too. But at Metro Bis, Chris is usually laid-back. The chefs gossip about the waitstaff, talk about their wives, and argue about where MSG comes from. We don't use it, but the Chinese restaurant that Alex ate in last night nearly killed him. (But he just can't live without the pork dumplings.)

The afternoon is a time for gossip. Even though chefs don't get out of the kitchen very often, there is a network of restaurant rumors that travel between employees and salesmen. Some of these stories become legends, like the one about the line cook somewhere in New York State who came to work in the morning, went to light the stoves, and blew the building up. There was an empty swimming pool below the kitchen that had filled with leaking gas during the night. There is also the rumor of the two Chinese chefs who stabbed each other to death after an argument about money, and the chef convicted of attempted murder after throwing hot Fry-O-Lator oil at his sous-chef. One of my favorite restaurant stories is about a couple living somewhere in the Caribbean. They were both chefs, and the woman had a better job than the man. This must have bothered him because he killed her and buried her in the backyard. Her employer soon called to find out why she hadn't come to work. The man explained that she had moved back to the United States and said he would love to have her job. Two weeks later while he was chopping vegetables in the middle of the kitchen, the police arrested him. Apparently the neighbors thought it odd for him to rent a backhoe and use it in the middle of the night. It doesn't matter if these tales are true because they provide for interesting discussion during the afternoon and good reasons to avoid violence while at work.

There are many unwritten rules in the kitchen. It is most important to clean your work area after each project and to work quickly and carefully. If you are talking and not working, you'll soon find yourself looking for a new job. And never, ever steal someone else's prep work and use it as your own. Smoke will blast from Chris's ears as if he were a cartoon character if a line cook walks in the fridge and uses the diced onion and celery that he was going to use.

The prep work is efficiently completed in the afternoon. It never ceases to amaze me when I find an item I thought would have been limited to one purpose being used in the kitchen. We have a wood file that is used for zesting lemons, a blowtorch for crème brûlée, PVC pipes for sculpting food, and an ultrabright five-hundred-watt lightbulb in the walk-in just in case someone needs to perform surgery. Plastic wrap, salt, chef coats—nothing in sight is out of the question when a problem needs to be solved.

"Are you using that toothpick for anything right now?"

"Can I borrow that soup ladle for just a minute?"

"Quick, get me a five-gallon bucket!"

Chefs are the most resourceful people in the world. When a refrigerator breaks down, Chris can be found, paring knife in hand, on his hands and knees peering into the unit. I once saw him use butcher twine to hold a wedding cake upright at a catering event. He never travels without duct tape (which can fix anything), a knife (the ultimate tool), and an extension cord (it's all about power). But I never let Chris loose in a hardware store because he would walk out with hundreds of dollars' worth of toys.

There are so many uses for plastic wrap beyond the standard purpose of covering food. It can be used as a lid above a pot of water to make it boil faster, as a belt to hold up chef pants if the elastic breaks, or as a mask to protect one's eyes when slicing onions. I've seen plastic wrap used to hold tablecloths in place at windy picnics, and I've heard that a whole roll can be used to restrain a line cook if enough people sneak up behind him.

Salt is also one of the more versatile ingredients in a

kitchen. I once watched in horror as the tray that catches the flotsam and jetsam from the pans on the stove caught on fire. Apparently it had not been cleaned the night before. Fire shot up between all of the burners and the entire stove looked like it might explode. I froze on the other side of the line in the middle of lunch and watched the flames in slow motion. The lunch cook panicked and was about to pull the chain to release the fire-suppressant system when Chris calmly grabbed the salt. He carefully pulled out the tray and smothered the flames with half of a box. When the fire was gone, the tray was slid back under the burners until lunch was over and it could be cleaned.

Salt has other uses, too. When a pan filled with butter to cook the goat cheese tarts was overturned on the floor in the middle of dinner, a layer of salt was applied and service didn't skip a beat. When the parking lot is too icy for someone to get safely to the Dumpster with the garbage, salt is scattered across the pavement. At the beginning of service each night, salt is sprinkled on the ice in hotel pans (picture the metal containers that fit in chafing dishes; they have many uses in the kitchen) to keep the inserts from sliding and spilling. (There isn't enough refrigeration on the line, so the chefs put the ingredients they will constantly need on ice within easy reach.)

Salt is essential but a chef's knives are sacred. One must guard his knives as if his life depends on it. Knife borrowing isn't as rampant in Chris's kitchen as it has been in other places he's worked. He has a very small kitchen with only a handful of employees and enough good-quality knives. Most places make chefs bring in their own, or they provide knives that are warped and can't be sharpened anymore. All of Chris's knives have his initials carved into the blade so other chefs from the restaurants he used to work in couldn't claim his knives as their own.

He used to go to great lengths to protect all of the equipment he used even if it didn't belong to him. At Mark's Place Chris used to fill his assigned metal inserts with food scraps at the end of each day and put them in the walk-in. In the morning, he dumped out the garbage from each container, washed them, and used them on his side of the line. There were never enough inserts for everyone else, but Chris always had his station ready to go.

When I met Chris the trunk of his car was loaded with side towels. The owner of the restaurant was cheap and never ordered enough, so Chris would hide them just in case the kitchen ran out before the next linen delivery. He hid tartlet pans in the freezer so there would be enough when it was his turn to make dessert. And he still has a thing with markers and pens. I'm not sure why, but he can never have enough writing implements. He protects all of the pens in the kitchen from the other chefs and waitstaff by putting them in his pockets during the day. At the end of the night, he unloads his loot in the living room. The next day this stockpiling game starts all over again. There are three fewer pens than the day before, so competition for writing implements is fierce.

Pens aren't the only restaurant items that end up at home. Before we opened Metro Bis, Chris bought small used kitchen equipment such as sheet pans, spoons, whisks, and hotel pans from an old guy with a beat-up truck. This guy would buy everything at auction, then wander around to different restaurants in the state selling his goods. Chris gathered these items and stored them under our bed for months. I swear that the bedroom was twenty degrees colder because of it.

Chris also feels the world is his napkin. It is rare to see him in a suit, because like most chefs, he is intensely uncomfortable in formal clothing. That's why he doesn't work a nine-to-five job, and it's another one of the reasons he dropped out of engineering school. Chris believes that all clothing was really intended to be a side towel. Anything that is absorbent can be and should be used to clean up a variety of messes. Spilled coffee all over the floor? This sweatshirt looks as though it can handle the mess. Got something sticky on his hands? The brand-new dress pants that Chris is wearing for the first time should be able to keep his hands clean and dry. Sometimes I find pairs of socks with wine stains on the bottoms. They truly are the quicker picker-uppers if you're not wearing any shoes. My greatest hope for an invention of the twenty-second century is affordable, disposable chef clothing.

I will never really understand Chris's work behavior. I just haven't put in enough hours in a kitchen. A sous-chef should be the chef's wife. They spend more time together than is normal or healthy. They love and hate each other but couldn't function well without each other. It's hard to describe a relationship based on ten to twelve hours a day of intense interaction. I wouldn't want to spend that much time with Chris. We would never get along. An excellent sous-chef is the chef's third hand and feels like an extension of the chef. It is an intuitive position, and a good sous-chef will know what the chef expects without his having to verbalize it. The sous must be able to translate the chef's food in a way that works for both of them. He must maintain his own creativity and drive while working under the direction of the chef. When the chef can hardly function because he hasn't had enough sleep and can't form a coherent sentence, the sous-chef is responsible for getting the job done. There is the potential for lots of conflicts if the chef's orders are not relayed properly to the rest of the kitchen staff, and their personality types must be well matched or they'll kill each other. In a faithful chef and sous-chef relationship, there's a bond that makes it so they are willing to go above and beyond for each other. The chef will bail his sous out of jail. The sous will work extra hours when the chef goes on vacation.

Chris has had two sous-chefs since opening Metro Bis. Al was with him for three years, and Norman currently fills the position. These two sous-chefs couldn't be more different, but they have both worked well with Chris. Al is very creative and has a good sense of taste. He and Chris spent lots of time exploring and experimenting with the menu. When Al came back from a trip to Korea, they worked together to incorporate the new flavors in the existing entrées. Norman is organized and trained in high-volume restaurants. He helps Chris plan the prep schedule, systematizes the storage room, and places orders with the purveyors. He delegates the workload to the rest of the kitchen staff and maintains order when Chris is not present.

Chris worked with one sous-chef before Metro Bis who was so concerned with pleasing him that he actually cooked potatoes for me in the middle of a busy lunch. When I had asked for fresh potatoes, I meant the ones from the fridge instead of the yellowish ones in the steam table. He misunderstood my request and cooked my potatoes to order.

The sous-chef also understands that the chef's first and foremost priority is feeding the public—not the wife. Nothing is more important. Nothing. Middle of a Saturday night and you just found out that your father has been in a car accident? Is he still alive? Yes? Then take this food to table four. The pope has made a special trip to your restaurant and would like to meet the chef. Sorry, there're too many tickets hanging. He's just going to have to wait. About to give birth on New Year's Eve? You'd better hold that kid in there until at least the second. This thought process has probably ended many marriages.

Chris forgot my birthday this year, but I didn't really care. I was just testing him in one of those barbaric female displays that I normally avoid. I wanted to see how many days or weeks would go by before he noticed that the date had passed. He had claimed to finally memorize my birth date, but I didn't believe him. I thought that it might be amusing to find out if he really would remember, knowing it would be easy to forget my Saturday-night birthday. I kept my mouth shut all day long. I didn't tell anyone except for a table of regular customers. The wife almost blew it. She was very upset that he hadn't remembered and she didn't understand my disturbing glee. She looked at him pointedly when he stopped by the table and said, "Are you doing anything special with Courtney tomorrow?"

He looked at me, I stopped glaring at her for a moment, and he said, "No, we'll probably just go out to dinner like we normally do but nothing special. Why?"

Her husband elbowed her in the ribs and she replied, "No reason. I was just wondering what you were doing tomorrow."

After surviving that close call, I thought I was all set to make it for a few days before he realized that he had forgotten my birthday. I would have been fine if he hadn't checked the e-mail as we sat in the office at eleven-thirty that night.

"Hey, Kate sent you one of those computer cards. I wonder why?" he said.

I held back my sarcasm and said sweetly, "Gee, I don't know," and waited for his expression when he opened the card. The best part was that his birthday is a month after mine, and I didn't have to get him a thing.

Chefs forget your birthday and often don't celebrate the holidays, but what has always fascinated me is their ability to ignore pain. I was watching a TV program about the New York City restaurant Gramercy Tavern last week, and one of the line cooks said that the only way he would be excused from service was if he chopped off one of his fingers. I once saw a guy fall down a flight of stairs in the middle of dinner at the restaurant I met Chris in. The guy had blisters the size of quarters on his back from falling asleep in the sun the day before. I told Chris that the guy was lying on the stairs.

"Is he okay?" Chris asked.

"He hasn't gotten up yet," I replied.

"Let me know if he's okay. Picking up one salmon, a Pad Thai, a medium steak, and a penne pasta. Ordering two baby greens, one spring roll, and a spinach salad."

Before I made it back to the stairway, the line cook had managed to roll over, crawl up the steps, and limp back in the kitchen.

"Sean, are you okay? Did you get the leg of lamb? Santiago, get five lamb. Sean, do his desserts."

Service kept on rolling.

It wouldn't be the last time that I would see something like that. Chris had pneumonia for ten weeks one winter. He never missed a day of work; instead he would choke down his pills followed by a handful of Tylenol. I asked him why he never took a day off when he had been sick, and he looked at me as if I were stupid.

"Why would I take a day off when I'm sick? I'd rather be at work when I'm sick and take a day off when I'm well enough to have fun."

He wasn't contagious, and he washes his hands an average of eighty-five times a day. I know that number because the waiters at his last job took bets and counted.

Pain is not allowed in the restaurant unless it can actually be seen. Chris had a friend who stabbed himself in the arm when cutting fish one day. The blood spurted from his vein like you'd expect to see in a Monty Python movie. He stared at the red geyser with quiet bemusement until someone reacted with a towel and drove him to the emergency room. This kind of pain is acceptable in the kitchen. You can see it. You know it must hurt.

Unseen pain doesn't count. Take, for example, the day Al, our last sous-chef, was struck down by a stalactite of ice hanging from the sprinkler valve in the walk-in freezer. I was working in Metro Express and he called to yell at me, saying I should call the building manager and have the sprinkler fixed. I told him the manager's number was on the refrigerator upstairs. He hung up on me.

Several hours later the dinner waitstaff found Al hunched over a table in the dining room. He was dizzy and had a headache. A waiter called me in Metro Express and told me I should come up and look at the chef's head. Why should I look at his head? Shouldn't he be able to determine whether or not his head was okay? Wasn't it his head? Better yet, wasn't he supposed to be in charge of the kitchen? What if someone else had hit her head? Would the chef have been able to deal with the situation? I called Chris at home and told him he had to come back to work. None of the prep for dinner had gotten done because the chef was dealing with his head.

When Chris came back he looked at the chef's head. There was blood. You could see the injury. It must have hurt. If it felt that bad, the chef should have gone to the walk-in clinic. I often wonder what life was like prior to the walk-in clinic. I'm sure that chefs frequently bled to death.

It turns out he had a concussion. In the morning he went to a second doctor for another opinion. Yep, it was a concussion, and he was mad at me for not coming upstairs to see his head. When he made it back to work three days later, he asked if I wanted to see the crater that had been drilled into his scalp.

Annoyed, I looked at him and said, "Will your crater hold water?"

"No," he replied.

"Then I don't want to see it," I said.

It's not that I didn't feel bad about his injury, and Al is a great guy, but I was annoyed by his inability to assess his condition and take some kind of action. I also felt a little guilty for not taking care of him.

The kitchen staff can be especially cruel when they feel that an injury is not substantial. After one of our line cooks burned the top of his hand in the late afternoon, he took a trip to the pharmacy for twenty-five dollars' worth of bandages, wraps, and creams before returning to the kitchen.

"Wow, I haven't burned myself like this in a long time," he said. "It hurts like a bitch."

Our six-foot-four sous-chef looked down at him. "Do you want me to kiss it? I can kiss it for you if you want me to. My six-year-old daughter says I have magic kisses. Whenever she gets a boo-boo, I kiss it for her; she says it makes her feel better. Are you sure you don't want me to kiss that for you?"

I once watched Jerry walk through the kitchen right after a waiter cut his finger on a glass while I was wrapping him with a Band-Aid.

"I cut myself on that glass, Jerry," the waiter announced.

"If it's not wiggling on the floor, then I don't want to hear about it," Jerry responded while he unloaded the dirty dishes he was carrying into the dishwashing station.

Delayed, long-term pain is also not acceptable.

When a waiter fell down a flight of stairs at home after he had been drinking, he missed two days of work. Then he complained about shooting pain in his arms and legs for the next two weeks, even though he didn't have a problem moving around during his shift. Every time that he worked, he would complain to anyone who would listen. Eventually someone told him he should go to the doctor. After all, it might be a tumor. He missed another day of work to go to the doctor and called in a panic to say he needed an MRI. He'd had three scheduled days off earlier in the week when he could have gone to the doctor, but he decided to go on a Friday. Once he was back at work, the sky truly must have been falling because he was convinced that he had slipped a disc and was stressed about how he was going to pay for the MRI, all of his money having been spent on alcohol.

Soon no one believed the boy who cried "wolf," and the staff quickly found that they, too, were in need of medical treatment.

"Oh no, I've burned myself. It has permeated my bones. I'll never be able to use my hand again. I need an MRI."

"No, you can't have an MRI yet. You need to wait for two weeks so that you have plenty of time to make everyone feel sorry for you."

"You're right. I'll go to the bar instead."

Most chefs know that the job needs to get done no matter what. They wrap some gauze and a few Band-Aids around their hands and get back to work. Other line cooks suck it up and ignore the pain because they fear the chef.

Some chefs rule by fear. They intimidate the waitstaff. They scream obscenities at dishwashers. Or they throw things like dish racks and escargot dishes. When I first met Chris he ruled with a quiet insanity. He never yells or swears, but employees are a little afraid of him. On slow nights in a prior kitchen Chris and his sous-chef would dress up a bread roll with eyes, nose, mouth, hair, and sometimes legs and arms, depending on the size. They would pretend that this piece of bread was the owner and would stab it repeatedly, sauté it, fry it, or boil it to death during service, much to the horror of the waitstaff and to the amusement of those in the kitchen. I thought that it was funny, too, and would stay in the kitchen while the rest of the waitresses ran back onto the floor shaking their heads. What did make me a little nervous, however, was what he called the lamb splitter. It was a huge knife with an odd hole in the end. It looked more like a machete to me. They used it when breaking down a whole leg of lamb into serving pieces. The key to using the lamb splitter was to wave it over your head, smile like Satan, and break through the bone on the first hit. This action was usually accompanied by some sort of heavy-metal rock music that your grandfather said you would go deaf listening to. The scene, needless to say, was always disturbing.

I have never been afraid of Chris, and I think that he liked that. I knew that it was all just a big show. There was something on the outside that told me he just liked playing with people, liked to try to get a reaction. Just like the quintessential middle child pestering his siblings. Every once in a while he tries it again. To poke me while I'm down. Like a cat who has just got a mouse. He always regrets it in the long run, but he still has to give it a try.

Another bothersome and intimidating scare tactic that Chris used was to refuse to learn a person's name until he had been working for more than six months. "Hey, you! You over there by the bread station! Yes, you. What's your name? Okay, Jeff, take this to table three. You'll find it. Out of the kitchen!"

It might have been Jeff's first day or his fifty-first; it didn't matter. Chris's stated excuse for not learning people's names was that the turnover was so high that he would be wasting his time. I am sure that it was just his way of teaching new people about the structure of the restaurant.

Chris also made sure to frequently talk about butchering—the human body. It is well known among chefs, butchers, farmers, doctors, and veterinarians that the human body is not much different from the bodies of every other animal on the planet. Each leg has five main muscles that make it move regardless of what species it is attached to. Break down a leg of lamb, veal, or bear, and it's pretty much the same. Rabbits without skin and heads are so similar to cats that they must have their kidneys intact when sold so that chefs can tell the difference. This realization of basic anatomy causes most chefs to wonder. Just how long would it take to break down a human body into servable parts?

What animal meat would human flesh be closest to? Would it be fatty or lean? Would it be best with the infamous fava beans and Chianti or with fiddleheads and Cabernet? Conversations like these happen with some regularity in restaurant kitchens. Chris used to discuss this terrifying subject whenever he wanted the waitstaff to leave him alone so he could finish his prep work.

Intimidation is often used in traditional kitchens as a way for the staff to understand where they fit in the hierarchy, and for the chef to maintain control. At the bottom of the pile is the unpaid or underpaid intern who has some education and is trying to gain experience before venturing out on his own. Norman, our sous-chef, completed his internship in New York City at Aureole. During his first day there Norman encountered the morning sous-chef, nicknamed the pit bull by the kitchen staff. He had earned his name by enforcing the standards of Charlie Palmer, the well-known chef/owner of Aureole, and his executive sous. These two men would wander through the kitchen giving tips on the proper plate design for each menu item. Whenever they noticed a line cook with a sloppy technique, they would inform the morning sous-chef of their displeasure and "sic" him on the unwitting kitchen worker. One day the pit bull stopped by Norman's station to check on his prep work. It had just taken him twenty minutes to slice a lemon rind as thinly as possible into strips. The pit bull stood next to Norman and massaged the lemon.

"I want it as fine as human hair," he hissed into Norman's ear as he threw the rind away.

Then he said more loudly so everyone in the kitchen could hear, "Have you paid your tuition yet, or are you on financial aid?"

Norman told the pit bull he had already paid.

"Good, then you can take the train back to school and ask the administration for your money back, because you haven't learned a thing," he responded.

The kitchen staff exploded in laughter, but by the end of the shift they would all fantasize about wrapping the pit bull in a blanket, beating him senseless, and leaving him across the street in Central Park. Norman did his best to stay out of the sous-chef's way, quickly learned where he stood in that kitchen, and survived his internship.

Chris's leadership style has changed a lot since he first started, and he never earned himself a nickname. It doesn't take too long to realize that most people work better when you don't scream at them. The more you yell, the more likely they are to make more mistakes. Chris is much more comfortable in his own restaurant. He doesn't have to compete with anyone but himself. He has the power to make all of the decisions, and he's more confident. Chris knows everyone's names, and the lamb splitter lays at rest in a kitchen drawer. There is no need to prove his leadership; he's the owner now. If the line cooks have a problem with his authority, then they can leave. Chris talks more to his staff and tries to get the most out of them. He wants them to strive for their best, and he knows he needs them to get the job done. He has the ability to work with them as a group and encourage them toward greatness under his rules. I think that they respect that and understand what he expects from them in return.

The kitchen staff respects me, too, but in a different way. They have a vague understanding of what I do, but they often think of me as a secretary or merely as Chris's wife. They are also puzzled by my vegetarianism. They just don't get it, and they enjoy kidding me about it.

"Hey, Courtney, I made cheeseburgers for staff meal. Do you want one?"

"I'd love a cheeseburger," I reply. "But I really don't like cheese. Can you take it off and add some bacon instead?"

Norman really tries to give me a hard time. During our last wine dinner I wandered through the kitchen just as they finished plating the foie gras course.

"Courtney, I saved some goose liver for you," Norman joked.

"No thanks," I replied.

"Why not? It's vegetarian."

"Uh-huh."

"Seriously. It's just corn filtered through a duck."

As the kitchen burst into laughter, I said, "I know they nail their feet to the floor and force-feed them with a tube."

"They don't nail their feet down anymore in the United

States, but I think they still do it in Israel. They must have the best foie gras ever. Can't get it in this country, though."

I know that he thinks I'm a freak, and I can't blame him. Norman works with meat all day long. The closest that I come to hunting is to kill a Christmas tree each year. Now, I'm no tree-hugging, pot-smoking druid, but I always feel a little bad. What right do I have to stomp through a field, saw in hand, and hack the life out of a defenseless tree? Chris thinks that I'm insane.

You can't image my horror when I watched him clean crabs for the first time, or cook lobsters, or tell the bunny story. Chris told me the bunny story many years ago when we were first forming a relationship. I was very curious about what he did, the way that he manipulated foods, and created flavor combinations. One of the things that bothers him most about a chef is when he doesn't have respect for the food. Chris says he can tell the chef who has been to the slaughterhouse from the one who hasn't. The chef who has seen the dead cows hanging from the hooks handles the meat carefully. He doesn't throw it around or play with it. The slaughterhouse chef is bothered when a product goes to waste not only because the food cost goes up, but because a life has been lost. A sacrifice has been made for nothing.

This is one of the reasons Chris went and killed the rabbits himself, so he would have a better appreciation of the life lost. The woman who owned the farm didn't have time to kill the rabbits and didn't like to do it. Chris didn't like to do it, either, but he had designed a rabbit entrée for the weekend specials. I'm glad that I didn't see him do it (apparently rabbits make a screaming noise just before they are slaughtered); I might not have married him. I thought that he was strange and disturbed to want such a close connection to what he made. I was much happier eating from a box in those days. It wasn't until years later when chef Thomas Keller's *The French Laundry Cookbook* came out that I felt relieved. Keller didn't want to kill the rabbits, either, but he did, and Chris didn't seem so disturbed to me anymore.

In the Bible there is a story of a starving man in the desert. He builds himself a fire and prays to God. A rabbit hops by and tells the man that he will sacrifice himself to feed him. The man gives thanks, appreciates the sacrifice, and is sad that this animal must die in order for him to live. A chef with an awareness of the sacrifices made has a deeper connection with himself and his food.

But killing rabbits didn't make Chris a vegetarian. And working at a macrobiotic restaurant during his internship in college didn't help, either. Being a vegetarian is too limiting for Chris, and he simply loves to eat meat. He doesn't get annoyed by vegetarians like some chefs do. He just doesn't get it. Sometimes I ask him why he has the right to take the life of another being in order to eat it. He looks at me as if I'm wearing an inner tube to a formal ball and says, "I'm at the top of the food chain. I didn't put us there, but it sure beats being at the bottom."

THE SCULPTOR
AND HIS CLAY

There are a number of privileges that come with being married to the chef. First of all I can eat during service. In the middle of a moderately busy lunch I can stroll into the walk-in, grab a yogurt, and crack it open on the other side of the line. I might chat with Chris as he feeds a table of six, then wander over to the dishwashing station so that the entire dining room can't see me eat. I very rarely sit down to dine except on Sundays. Most meals are eaten just prior to service. Usually I enjoy a cup of whipped potatoes as I walk to the bar to get a club soda in a beer glass with no ice. I usually get the hiccups on the way through the dining room because I'm eating too fast.

I don't eat the majority of what Chris makes. I'm much happier with some soup, a salad, some pasta, and yogurt. That's pretty much all that I eat. I once read that most people eat the same five things over and over. I know that's true in my case. Sure, I might enliven my potatoes with goat cheese and chives, or dine on purple ones or sweet, but it's all just potatoes.

In the beginning Chris was somewhat unnerved by my

eating habits. He wanted to be able to make me something that made me happy. The main goal of any chef is to please the customer. I wouldn't have any of it. He finally resigned himself to a limited understanding of my strange appetite, and it ended there. He never feels pressured to cook for me or worries about my opinion except for when he makes gnocchi. This is the only item that must pass my inspection. I rate each batch on a scale of one to ten, with ten being the highest. Most batches are an eight. He doesn't make gnocchi that often because I like to eat them all and they are a lot of work to make. I'm glad this is the only item where my opinion counts. I don't feel pressured to eat and he doesn't feel pressured to cook.

Sometimes I like to make Manchurian dip for myself when he doesn't have time. We used to go to an Indian restaurant on Sundays until it closed, and I would always order the nan breads with this dip. It's great on a baguette, too, and it's awesome on cauliflower. Just before the Indian chef left for a job in Canada, Chris got the recipe. Don't bother trying to make it without a food processor. It just won't come out right. The recipe will be more exact if a scale is used to weigh the ingredients, but I'd recommend using a prep cook or not bothering with the scale. It's a lot faster. So gather 1 large (5 ounces) carrot, 1 small green chili pepper, 1 medium ($3\frac{1}{2}$ ounces) red onion, 2 large stalks (3 ounces) of celery, 1 large bunch ($1\frac{3}{4}$ ounces) of cilantro, stems and all, 10 peeled cloves ($2\frac{1}{2}$ ounces) of garlic, 1 tablespoon of vegetable oil, 2 cups (1¼ pound) of ketchup, 2 ounces (just measure with a one-ounce ladle) of soy sauce, 1 tablespoon of sugar, 1 teaspoon of hot chili powder (or ½ teaspoon of cayenne), salt, and pepper. Clean and roughly chop the carrots, celery, onion, and cilantro if the dishwasher hasn't done it for you. Then throw them in the food processor with the garlic and chili pepper. While all that is pureeing, find a medium saucepan, dump the oil in it, and put it on medium-high heat. When the vegetables in the food processor are unrecognizable and just about liquid, put the mixture in the now-warm pan. Heat it until the entire neighborhood can smell the garlic and cilantro or until it's really bright green. This should take about three to four minutes. Add the ketchup and soy sauce, mix it, and leave it on the stove for another ten minutes with medium-low heat. (If the burner isn't turned down, the Manchurian dip will end up all over the stove while it sputters and spits.) When everything is starting to thicken and it's beginning to look like BBQ sauce, it's time to put in the sugar, chili powder, salt, and pepper. This is when I make Chris taste it; he adds more salt, which he tells me I need if I want it to be seasoned properly after it cools. Uh-huh. I want to eat it now. Take it off the stove, and eat it warm with some bread, or shrimp, or chicken, or whatever. Or enjoy it the "right" way after it has chilled in the fridge. I like it both ways. It tastes a little different when it's cold. Chris says it will live for one week in the fridge, but I always eat the full quart in two days. If it's busy in the kitchen and the line cooks are grumpy, then I clean up after myself. If not, I just wander into the dining room with the pot and a loaf of bread. It's one of my favorite kitchen meals enjoyed between lunch and dinner.

When I do sit down to eat in our restaurant, I can order almost anything that I want. I've had hard-boiled eggs, steamed broccoli, and ravioli, to name a few of the items regularly enjoyed, none of which reside on the menu. If I sat close enough to the kitchen, I could probably hear them grumble, so I sit as close to the bar as possible and order what I like. When I'm not pretending to be a customer, I usually fend for myself, which involves lots of soup, pasta, potatoes, and salad. I always ask for permission before I help myself. Taking food without asking can lead to a riot. Occasionally the kitchen will make gnocchi, which I love, but they try to hide them, hoping that I won't notice until they have all sold out. I normally discover the gnocchi half-way through their run, and I request them twice a day until they're all gone. If I'm really lucky, I'll get to have them twice in three days. Gnocchi are a pain to make, so I'm not allowed to eat them unless I'm playing customer. The only other menu item that I enjoy but can't have is the goat cheese tart, another labor-intensive item.

The funniest part is that the dishwashers get to eat whatever they want most of the time. Chris says that keeping the dishwashers happy is the key to a successful day. It is not uncommon for me to stand next to the dishwasher while she dines on a medium-rare steak with garlic whipped potatoes and a rosemary demi-glaze while I enjoy a bowl of buttered rice with cracked whole pepper. The dishwashers usually work harder than I do anyway, and I wouldn't want to eat a steak.

There are a few dishes that I love to eat, like truffled risotto—rich, creamy risotto with truffle butter, truffle oil, and fresh truffles shaved on top. We don't do this dish at Metro Bis because there aren't very many people in our area who would pay seventy-five dollars for rice. Even when it is the most perfect dish ever created on earth.

Besides, Chris loves to cook with fish. He loves intense flavors and comforting food. I once asked him if he thought his style of cooking was more feminine or masculine. I had read a cookbook where the chef discussed the gender of his own style. Chris thought his style was probably more feminine, although he didn't really care for sex being used as a description of food. His food is mostly light and mostly healthy. He doesn't use a lot of cream or butter and likes the natural flavors of the ingredients to come through.

One of the restaurant's most popular dishes is the pan-seared diver sea scallops with lobster whipped potatoes. (Diver sea scallops are gathered by hand from the bottom of the ocean by divers instead of by boats dredging everything off the seafloor.) Customers rave about the unusual potatoes and the sweet tenderness of the scallops. I often join in the conversation by agreeing that the scallop dish is phenomenal and very popular.

"I *love* the potatoes," I say. "I could eat them every night."

Actually, I've never even had them—they are loaded with *lobster*—but they don't look that bad.

Chris thinks of food as a malleable ingredient that can be manipulated to create a variety of flavors. For me, food is the product that we sell. If we eat it ourselves or throw it away before it gets to the table, we lose money. For Chris, food is an intricate combination of flavors in synchronicity on a plate. He tries to take the essence of the ingredients and make them more vibrant. He wants you to taste tomatoes, mushrooms, and lamb together and separately at the same time.

After Chris has a food-related dream, he'll leap out of bed, rush to the restaurant, and experiment with the items he combined in his sleep. He often tells me that he can think taste. He says most people can't do it. I know that I can't. Chris can read a cookbook, examine the ingredients, and taste the final product in his head. He knows what lobster and anchovies would taste like together, and he doesn't have to cook them to find out. One of the biggest problems in a commercial kitchen is that chefs don't taste. Not just with their minds but with their mouths. Most chefs don't eat the food they cook for everyone else. The kitchen becomes an assembly line of potato, vegetable, meat, sauce, and garnish. All the ingredients that form a dish need to be tasted throughout their production, but most chefs don't have time, don't care, or can't really taste. Chris tastes everything all day long. At night he'll sit on the couch while watching TV and say, "I'm fat."

I'll ask, "What did you eat today?"

"Nothing," he'll reply. Nothing to him means that he didn't actually make himself something to eat. He just tasted every single item that was produced in the kitchen that day. Chefs who don't taste their food come up with bizarre combinations like blueberry ketchup on steak and other tragedies.

The creation of a dish is a very personal expression of the chef's talent and taste. This is one of the reasons egos rage throughout the restaurant business. To insult a dish that a chef has spent his whole life and his cumulative experience creating is worse than saying his penis is two inches long with an inch-wide hairy mole on the side of it.

A culinary creation is like a painting. The flavors have been blended together like different shades of paint. The ingredients have been meticulously placed to appeal to all five senses. Cooking is one of the few professions that offers immediate validation. On a Thursday night you can see Chris peering out from the kitchen. He's watching the people on table six to see if they like his new appetizer. He's looking at the dinner plates on table nineteen to make sure they liked everything. Some chefs think about their mothers, grandmothers, or fathers when they cook. Chris looks out in the dining room and knows that he is cooking for the couple celebrating an anniversary on table three.

Customers have started to think about cooking as more than a way to satisfy hunger, too. I once was called over to a table where the customers wanted to debate whether cooking was a craft or an art. Chris vehemently defends cooking as a craft and feels that art is reserved for pastry chefs, whose work with sugar and chocolate rivals any with oil paint and plaster. This is probably a result of having watched his father create a village of gingerbread houses, perfect buttercream roses, and marzipan-covered cakes that looked like presents.

I don't think that the combination of ingredients on a plate is art; it is a craft. But the combination of flavors is completely different. Just the right amount of salt can bring out the soul of the tomato, the fullest flavor. Paired with an oaky aged balsamic vinegar, the flavor can take on new meaning. It doesn't happen every day, but when food inspires or induces thought beyond sustaining life, it can be artistic. This experience is so fleeting that it isn't often considered art.

This is why food memories are so important. I recently read an article about a man who was searching for the truffle taste of his youth, which he had experienced as a boy in Italy. He spent years trying to recapture that sensation, that odor, that fleeting feeling in his body. As his search proved unsatisfactory, the author wondered if the quality of truffles had decreased, if his childhood truffles had been tampered with and altered by truffle oil, or if his memory of those truffles was stronger than reality. Yes, he got all that from a stinky fungus.

Obviously food goes beyond sustaining life. It is more than a presentation on a plate. Everyone has a food they lust for but can't replicate. Everyone who cooks has a recipe that a friend used to make perfectly. It just can't be reproduced in the same way even if the friend really did provide the entire, correct recipe. There is more to food than ingredients. There are circumstances and company to take under consideration.

Chris unconsciously shares his philosophy with each bite. Food is a personal connection between people. He shares his childhood, his respect for the product, his love of food, and his philosophy of flavor with each person who dines. Yet customers still complain about a $19.95 steak.

Even with the diner's unconscious, personal connection with the chef, at the end of the day it really is just food, the fuel for the body. No one who hasn't worked in the restaurant business can truly understand what it takes to get dinner on a plate. Chris spends hours talking to purveyors, determining the quality of their goods, and bargaining for the best price. When the provisions arrive at the back door, they are inspected and returned if not up to Chris's standards. The acceptable products are then processed through the kitchen. The dishwasher might peel and chop. The prep cook might combine and mix. Everything is tasted along the way. Salt and pepper are added and more ingredients are combined. Some things are cooked days in advance while others are left until the last possible minute.

Customers and friends often ask me how everything can be ready at the same time. Timing is a learned skill. Cooks learn that potatoes take a certain amount of time and fish takes another. They keep adding items to their sense of timing and soon they have a natural, automatic response. Or they don't, in which case they will be yelled at by so many head chefs that they will probably find work in a lower-stress restaurant or consider a new career.

In Chris's case timing has been an invaluable skill. He can have six completely different pots on the stove while he talks on the phone, but he'll know when he needs to shut up and go stir the Israeli couscous. Oddly, this ability is not present anywhere else but in the kitchen. At home, if I ask Chris to take out the garbage and switch over the laundry, he'll completely forget what I told him and vacuum instead.

The timing skill in the restaurant has been very challenging for me. A chef prioritizes everything. He knows that it will take X amount of time to complete each task and exactly what time of the day the job needs to be done. Sometimes I'll walk into the kitchen at three P.M. on a Friday and Chris will be running around stressed because the kitchen is already in the weeds. They won't be ready for dinner service in two and a half hours unless they move. Any item not on the priority list doesn't get done.

This can be somewhat frustrating. When we first opened Metro Express, our takeout store, we couldn't find or really afford staffing. I worked every day from ten A.M. to seven-thirty P.M. by myself. Since I wasn't anywhere near the office, I couldn't complete my business tasks during the brief hours of nine to five Monday through Friday. I often asked Chris for help, only to be left frustrated. My tasks were not essential to the daily flow of the kitchen. Going to the post office or the bank didn't impact whether the food was prepped in time for dinner. My duties were not on the immediate priority list because they simply weren't essential to the moment. Eventually I felt nothing I did mattered, that my job wasn't as important as his. Not having the salmon portioned in time for dinner was more important than finishing payroll. Couldn't I just send in payroll later? There were people standing at the front door who might order salmon in the next ten minutes. What could be more important than that? One day as I sat in the office crying, with so much snot in my nose that I had to gasp through my mouth, I insisted that Chris really didn't care about me at all, and nothing I did mattered.

He looked at me incredulously and said, "How can you think that? If you don't do your job, then we would have no food. You don't really think that I could pay the bills, do you? I would probably lose half of the bills before they got to the office to be paid."

Even though I believed him, I still struggle with his priorities. Nothing, nothing, nothing is more important than the kitchen.

This is why I think about tattooing my birth date and wedding anniversary on his wrist. Chris works on a day-to-day basis. On Monday the food must be ordered, on Tuesday the food must be prepped, and on Wednesday and Thursday the kitchen must gear up for the weekend. On Friday and Saturday it's busy. Then the cycle starts all over again. Chefs spend all day long inside without windows. It is usually over 100 degrees in the kitchen. The passing of time is marked by lunch and dinner each day. The prep schedule keeps track of the day of the week. A chef will suddenly realize that it is no longer summer when he walks out of the restaurant in the middle of November and he's cold.

The seasons in the kitchen change with the ingredients. Soft-shelled crabs, asparagus, morel mushrooms, fiddleheads, corn on the cob, brandywine tomatoes, and butternut squash pass through on their way to the dining room. It's never spring, summer, fall, or winter. It's truffle season or time for the sweetest, plumpest scallops.

Since my time is marked with food, I've managed to learn a lot in spite of myself. I had no idea that saffron spice consists of the stigmas of the crocus flower. The three stigmas are separated from the flower by hand, and it takes thirty to forty of these little sterile sex organs to fill a half teaspoon. Saffron is harvested in Spain, India, and Iran, with a gram selling in the United States for ten dollars or more.

I also know now that fleur de sel is sea salt harvested from square beds on the shores of France. The majority of salt separated from seawater is called sel gris, and it's chunky and heavier than fleur de sel. For every eighty pounds of this salt, only one pound of fleur de sel is gathered. Fleur de sel is lighter and more fragrant. It rises to the top of the beds and is carefully skimmed off. This is considered the best salt in the world, and it is always added at the end of a dish's preparation so its aroma won't be lost during cooking.

I have learned about the different types of caviar: Sevruga, Osetra, Beluga, and 000 Beluga. If you are cool you pronounce the last one "triple-zero Beluga," not "zero, zero, zero." Then there are the other caviars, like cod roe, that can be eaten like a sausage in its egg sack, and Tobikko, which is often flavored with wasabi. Most of these eggs are taken from the fish on the boat (some are now farm raised). The fish are usually thrown back in the ocean dead, but some fishermen perform a kind of C-section and allow the fish to swim away. An expert salts the eggs, which preserves them for shipping all over the world.

Until I met Chris I really didn't know that people in

Colonial America wouldn't eat tomatoes because they thought they would die from the poisonous fruit, and they used corn cobs for toilet paper. I wish that I didn't know that sea urchins are edible, although it may be helpful if I'm ever stranded on a desert island. I was shocked to find dried grasshoppers in plastic potato-chip-style bags the first time I went to the Asian market with Chris.

Blowfish, or fugu, really puzzle me, too. I'm quite sure the people who eat it are totally insane. Some Japanese pay hundreds of dollars to eat this deadly fish to prove their virility and social status. There are only a handful of chefs in the world who are qualified to serve it. If they break any portion of the ovary, liver, or intestines, the adventurous diner will die. The Japanese are also known for Kobe beef. Really high-end restaurants import it to the United States, but it has been produced here for years. This breed of cow is different. From what I've heard, the cows are fed beer during the summer months to keep up their appetites. Now, here's the weird part. People wander among the cows and massage them with sake, a light Japanese alcoholic beverage. So the meat doesn't get tough, of course. It's safe to say that we have an odd relationship with our food.

PREPARING
FOR BATTLE

*E*ven though we work with it all day, Chris and I usually aren't thinking about food just before service. What we are focused on is people. People coming in for dinner. People who need specials. I'm usually in the office just prior to service, trying to finish up my paperwork. Today I'm trying to order a case of paper on-line. I like to wait until quarter of five because all of the office workers are getting ready to go home and the site works faster. I can hear the door to the shopping complex open and Chris race down the stairs. He's late again.

"I gotta do specials."

"Uh-huh. Just let me finish my order."

He hovers impatiently over my shoulder. Fifteen seconds pass while I punch in my credit-card number. "Are you finished yet? I'm running late."

"You're late every day, and you can see that I'm waiting for the computer to process my credit card."

"Okay, you're finished. Let me sit in the chair."

Chris sits down and checks the e-mail.

"I thought that you were running late," I grumble.

"I'm expecting an e-mail from Bill."

Chris soon realizes that there is no e-mail for him, so he opens Word and says, "Did I tell you that Lee called? She wants to have dinner this Sunday. Are we booked?"

I'm sitting on the other side of the desk flipping though a trade publication. I ignore him. He won't hear me when I respond anyway because he'll be busy typing the specials. If I do talk to him, he'll become distracted, unknowingly produce a hysterical typo, and print the menus with seared coed, wild stripped bass, or roasted lamb lion for the customers. I can't stand wasting paper no matter how hard the waitstaff laugh at the specials. Besides, he won't have any time to redo them, so I'll be back in the office fifteen minutes from now retyping the specials.

After Chris hits the print button, I respond. "I thought that we were booked for this weekend."

"Did you pay the bread bill?"

"No, I'm waiting for the weekly statement to be faxed."

"David called. Tell Jerry he's got a waiter running late."

"Did the dishwasher get fixed?"

"Yeah, it's going to be six hundred dollars for the part. Did you notice that we're out of shampoo?"

"There's more in the closet. We're out of toothpaste. I'll pick some up tonight."

"Chen can only work on Tuesdays from now on."

"I'll put an ad in tomorrow."

The printer winds down and we head upstairs.

"Did you check the e-mail?" Chris asks while opening the front door of the restaurant.

"You just did."

When we walk into the dining room, Dean is busy filling the sink at the bar with ice. He has all the wines by the glass on ice, too, and he'll take the drink garnishes out of the fridge in a minute. He's already swept, filled creamers, and switched the menu from lunch to dinner. All he has left to do is restock the takeout containers from storage, light the candles, and replace the napkins in the bread baskets. He looks up from his five-gallon bucket of ice as we walk in.

"Courtney, your mother called when you were in the office. Both lines were busy."

I thank him and head to the back phone. As I chat with my mother about her last tennis match and her assessors' deadlines, I glance into the kitchen. The tray with dinner items has been pulled from the fridge and some light prep work is being finished. Plum tomatoes are being sliced for roasting and the dishwasher is peeling potatoes for dinner tomorrow. There is light banter between the line cooks, Alex and Keith. They are being picked on for driving to and from work together. "So I hear you're a couple now," Jerry says as he walks in the back door. Jerry just finished dinner with his kids. He pauses on his way through the dining room, listens for a second to my conversation, realizes that it has nothing to do with business, and says, "I have a gift certificate that needs to be mailed this afternoon. I need another lesson on the postage meter."

I tell my mother I'll talk to her later and head back to the office with Jerry.

"Where's David?" he asks.

I unlock the office door for the two hundredth time today. "He called to say he's running late."

"If he's late because he's playing golf again, I'm going to kick his ass. I don't understand why he can't get off the course sooner."

I begin demonstrating the wonders of the postage machine. "Chris took the call."

"Great. He could have told Chris that he was going to be late because he scheduled a manicure at five o'clock, and Chris won't have even cared. I don't understand why this machine won't stamp when I put the envelope in."

"You should be glad that you even got your phone messages. There's an eight-top at six."

"I set it up before I left after lunch."

By the time we get back upstairs for service, Dean is folding napkins, David is putting on his tie in the middle of the dining room, the kitchen is debating whether sucking a cock now and then makes you a faggot, and the first table is getting out of their car in the parking lot.

3

ESCAPE

RUNNING FOR THE DOOR

*A*s I greet the first couple and show them to table one, I realize that Chris and I were supposed to have dinner together tonight. We were just going to grab a pizza, or Indian, or Mexican, but the reservations look pretty heavy and Chris is working on a catering job that is going out tomorrow. It's almost a relief to be working tonight. I'm not ready to drag Chris from the building. He always has just one more thing that has to get done before he leaves. "I forgot to put in a fish order." "I need to check on the key lime tarts." "I just need to make sure that the stock is ready to be put on later tonight." Then he needs to say good-bye to everyone and offer parting words of advice. "Make sure that you get started on that leg of lamb if you have time tonight." "You should send out an appetizer or dessert to Brian tonight. Make sure he's on a good table."

Jerry and Norman already know what they need to do, and Chris is just being annoying. Chris will make a trip to the car with his mysterious bag of papers, and Jerry will lock the door hoping that Chris won't come back in. Chris will just unlock the door, fill his cup of coffee, and tell them his cell phone number for the millionth time. Eventually I just get in the car, turn on some music, and Jerry shoves him out the side door. I never worry about the restaurant when we aren't there. I know that the key lime tarts will come out of the oven in time, and that if they don't, someone will remake them in the middle of service. Chris just needs to feel essential to the kitchen. It's hard for him to leave, which is why I'm relieved that he is too busy to remember the dinner out that he promised yesterday.

PLACES TO GO,
PEOPLE TO SEE

We don't usually leave the building during dinner service, anyway. When we do leave, we usually to go to a television studio, an Asian market, or another restaurant. Every once in a while we go someplace special like the James Beard Awards, a wine tasting, or an aquarium. And we have been known to take a vacation once a year.

Chris's first television appearance was on Channel 30 News, the NBC affiliate, when they used to run a cooking segment on the nine A.M. Sunday news. To be on live TV at 9:20, we had to get up at six A.M. after a Saturday night when we usually go to bed around one A.M. The first time we went, we stopped by the restaurant, picked up all of the food, and headed to the studio. We walked into the entry-way, or rather I walked while Chris and Al shuddered with fear, but the door was locked. Al had no intention of being on TV but had come along because he wanted to see the inside of a studio. Chris was obviously nervous and needed Al by his side. I guess it felt more like the restaurant kitchen that way.

We followed the instructions next to the studio phone and said, "Front door, please," incessantly until someone came to unlock the doors. A man greeted us with, "You here to do the cooking segment?" and led us into the studio. "This is the table," he grunted, and walked away. I set up the table as well as I could. I wasn't sure what to put on it. I didn't know what would show up well on camera. We had decided before leaving the restaurant to bring a large marble sculpture with us to be used as decoration. I placed it on the left-hand side of the table, which gave Al the perfect place to hide. He emerged once during the less than three minutes Chris was on air to flip three corn cakes before they had finished cooking, then retreated behind his marble facade. Chris fumbled through the rest of the demonstration. He didn't know when the segment was supposed to start or end. In a breath it was over (two minutes and thirty-four seconds goes really fast), and we were told to pack up quickly and quietly because the adopt-a-pet piece would be on next.

After that glorious morning I sent Chris for media training and he improved phenomenally. He soon became a regular guest at Channel 30 News, appearing every three weeks until there was a change in the production staff and the segment was canceled.

One Sunday morning, though, I dragged Chris to the shower, turned on every light in the house, and got ready to go to the restaurant. Chris stumbled from the shower to the bedroom, got dressed, and went to his car. I ran behind him with his dry-cleaned and pressed Egyptian-cotton chef coat, which I still don't trust him with alone. While I locked the house, he backed out of the driveway and began to drive away without me. At six-thirty on a Sunday morning I stood in the middle of the street screaming obscenities that he could hear through the car glass and threw down that precious chef coat. Chris slammed on the brakes, but before he could turn around, I ran back to the house, locked the door, and put up the chain. As he hurled his body against the door in an effort to regain access to our apartment, I lay underneath the blankets of the bed sobbing. After breaking the chain, he leapt up the staircase, burst into the bedroom, and tried to coax me to the car. I told him he could go do his own fucking TV show. He insisted that he couldn't go without me. I told him I wasn't going. He said that he wasn't going, either. I eventually relented and sat stiffly in the passenger seat of the car.

"I'm tired," he whined. "I didn't mean to forget you. I thought that I was going to work, and you never go to work with me."

"You suck, I hate you, and I hope you make an ass out of yourself on TV." I was too tired to maintain my silence for much longer. When we arrived at the studio, we were managing civil speaking terms, and he did complete the segment without making an ass out of himself.

This led to more TV appearances, including two half-hour shows for a local cable company. Usually I help Chris to set up the segments and get organized before the taping. One time I was with a friend, so I left him on his own. Instead of setting up I just watched the show. After they finished taping the first show, I asked the host if he could tap Chris's foot a minute before the show would be going to commercial. It was clear to me that Chris was unsure about how much more time he had. He didn't know if he should be throwing everything together or taking his time. The host explained to me that the show wasn't like that and he decided when he would be going to commercial. Then he said that Chris was the star of the show tonight and that I should just leave him alone. "Chris is the star every night," I said under my breath.

The host followed me into the control room asking, "Who runs the restaurant? Who runs the kitchen?"

I did my best to ignore him so that he would just go away. At the end of the second segment he approached me and asked sarcastically, "Did he do okay? Was the show good enough for you?"

I left and sat in the car while Chris loaded everything. He didn't understand why I was upset.

"He was probably just kidding," he said.

"That's nice. I'm never coming back here again."

I will probably go back at some point, if we are invited. I try to go on all of his work-related trips, including his frequent stops at ethnic markets. Chris can't drive by one without stopping for at least an hour. I can't even imagine what it must be like to eat seaweed or bugs. It is easy to lose Chris in one of these stores for hours. When we have to get supplies, I just stay in the car and take a nap. He pokes the produce, examines the live fish, and tries to read each of the thousands of containers that line the shelves. As far as I know he can't read Chinese, Japanese, Vietnamese, or Thai. In an ethnic market Chris is truly happy.

I love going to the grocery store. I only get to go there once or twice a month, and I love to buy products I can't get from the restaurant, like frozen ravioli, canned soup, and cereal. I could live on cereal. Chris once tried to order some through the restaurant, but it came in such a large package that I couldn't eat it all before it went stale.

Chris doesn't go to the grocery store that often—maybe five or six times a year—since most of his time is spent chained to the stove. He's used to squeezing, smelling, and then screaming about his produce every morning in the restaurant. I don't want a scene like this in the grocery store. For example, when Chris is planning a five-course dinner in the restaurant, he will tear open each box of produce in the morning. He may discover that the bean sprouts he ordered as a garnish for the main dish have formed a juicy, rotten mass. He pokes the sprouts, puts his hand in them to make sure they all have the same degree of slime, tells the driver to take "this nasty-ass excuse for sprouts" back, and then gets on the phone. Chris starts by indicating his intense displeasure to his salesman, who should have known that this was a very important dinner and should have selected the sprouts personally from the warehouse floor. When the salesman insists that the sprouts were fine when they left this morning, Chris asks to speak with the manager. (If we're lucky, this phone conversation will happen prior to lunch service. I've actually had a customer tell me that he doesn't want to hear about the slimy chives, bean sprouts, and raspberries while he is eating.) If Chris is successful, the salesman will drive forty minutes with the freshest, most beautiful sprouts that he has ever seen or will ever see again.

My point? Even if the grocery store produce came from the same purveyor we use, it would never be up to the chef's standards. If I really want to buy a bunch of grapes from the grocery store, I will go alone. Chris will poke them, taste them, decide they aren't good enough, and insist I not buy them. If I insist that the grapes are worthy of my consumption, then I will be insulted for my lack of taste and he will offer a lengthy explanation in the middle of the grocery store as to why these grapes are inferior. His sous-chef would absolutely agree with him, and I should, too.

While he may get away with quietly ranting about the produce in the grocery store, it is not okay to comment on the food at another person's restaurant. When a confident, non-ego-driven chef dines at another restaurant, he doesn't want to be noticed. Nothing is more irritating than going to a restaurant with your mother, who must announce to the waitress that she is waiting on a chef. The waitress's response will usually be a look that says, "I don't give a shit who you are." A real chef wants to have a genuine, private dining experience. On days off he usually just wants to be left alone. If he wanted to be fawned over, he would go to a restaurant where he already knows the chef.

There are unwritten rules to follow when dining at another restaurant as an identified chef, like Chris. Most chefs, regardless of how well we know them, will send out a free sample or appetizer at the beginning of the meal as a gesture of camaraderie. If we are in a restaurant where we have a closer relationship, then the entire meal will be comped. In exchange, we feed those chefs and/or owners for free when they come to our restaurant. This tends to be a good situation for both parties unless the one chef always provides a free meal but never goes to the other chef's restaurant. This is extremely offensive to the dining chef because it makes him feel guilty about eating for free at a restaurant he obviously likes. It also makes him wonder if the other chef doesn't like the food he serves. It is also important in a comped situation to tip unusually high. This is because your meal is free, and because a chef in the business should understand the plight of the wait staff.

I once had a restaurant emergency when out to dinner with a friend. We were eating at the bar, when the bartender recognized me as Chris's wife. He informed the kitchen of my presence, and the chef sent out a fabulous gazpacho soup with raw oysters lurking in its depths. I panicked. I didn't know what to do. Chefs usually examine these plates when they go back to the kitchen. Ours would be left untouched because my friend and I don't eat oysters. I couldn't insult the chef. I twisted back and forth in my bar stool and decided the best way out of my situation was to murder the bartender and spill the soup in the process. I called Chris instead and pleaded with him to join us for dinner.

"I can't go anywhere. It's busy," he said.

"What should I do with the soup?"

"Have the bartender wrap it up to go at the bar. Why are you so worried about this?"

"How would you feel if you sent something out for free and no one even touched it?"

"I think I'd get over it."

"You don't understand. You always eat what the chefs make for you."

"Okay, I gotta go."

"I'm bringing home this oyster soup."

"Whatever. Bye."

Chris claimed not to have understood, but I know that he did. Whenever a nonvegetarian item is offered to us, he eats mine and his even if he doesn't really care for it. To not eat another chef's dishes while in his restaurant is the greatest insult that one chef can give another. The bread can be completely charred, the lettuce doing the breast stroke in three inches of dressing, and the pasta cooked to mush, but unless the chef fears death by eating the meal, he will deliberately suck it all down.

We had a meal once at a local restaurant where we knew the owner a couple of years ago. She sat with us during our lunch and chatted about business, employees, and customers. I don't remember what Chris ordered, but he politely managed to eat his meal. I wasn't as lucky. The grilled cheese I had ordered was black on the bottom. (Probably a new chef who hadn't learned my microwaving secret yet.) The pasta salad that came with my sandwich was loaded with chicken. No mention of chicken on the menu, but there was definitely chicken on my plate. The owner asked if everything was okay.

"I actually just ate," I said, "but Chris wanted to go out. I'm really full, but it's really good. I'll take it to go."

Chris just smiled. "Mine couldn't have been any better."

He learned this line from a chef friend who found a good way to comment on a meal without being insulting. Marco Pierre White captured the reason that chefs don't tell one another when something is wrong with their food when he wrote in his cookbook *White Heat*, "If I came to your house for dinner an hour late, then criticized all your furniture and your wife's haircut and said all of your opinions were stupid, how would you feel?" Chefs understand that they are guests in someone's house. Chris hardly even comments on another chef's cooking unless he is working in our kitchen.

This is why it is a tremendous relief to be an anonymous diner or to eat in an exceptional restaurant. Last year Chris and I ate at the French Laundry. On our way to dinner we found ourselves in the rental car three thousand miles from home debating whether we should keep our reservation. We often have arguments over things we actually agree on. Chris and I will argue the same point from different aspects of the issue to the death. As we spoke of our expectations for this extraordinary restaurant, we were tense. I didn't want to go to the restaurant because I had a concept of what a great restaurant should be, and I didn't want it to be crushed by reality. I didn't want to be disappointed. I wanted my abstract concept of excellence to remain intact. I wanted something to continue to strive for. I didn't want to lose my motivation for my own business over one meal.

Chris wanted to know if all the hype was true. What makes a restaurant famous? Food writers. Who are the food writers? People with opinions. Chris wanted to know if the French Laundry really was about the food. Can a restaurant achieve a national reputation through networking with only average food? Would the food live up to its reputation? There are several restaurants in New York City that have lowered their standards. They serve mediocre food to hoards of tourists looking for a name-brand dining experience. (There's nothing wrong with that. They're making more money than I ever will.) Would the French Laundry be the same?

As we settled into the table, the conversation in the car simply slipped away. It was just Chris and me eating in yet another restaurant. Service was friendly, helpful, and attentive. The food met all of my expectations, but my standards were so high, they could have never been exceeded. There was something disturbing, though, and it's probably because I don't go to church. The room was almost silent. There was none of the usual background music. No artwork on the walls. Everything was a different shade of beige. We were compelled to whisper, and I was glad in the end that our company was unable to join us. It would not have been the same experience. There would have been the distraction of conversation that the French Laundry obviously attempts to avoid. I had the distinct impression that chef Keller would have preferred to have all tables for one so that his food would gain the attention that was clearly desired. The reverent quiet of the place was almost as if some monks from Tibet had joined us for dinner. They would chant their prayers, then stop and contemplate their words. We would dine, the plates would be cleared, and we would sit quietly savoring the last course while anticipating the next during the full three- to five-minute interval between plates. Despite my attempts to lighten the atmosphere with cracks about wanting to be a food walker (rather than a runner) and the staff-selection process being based on one's ability to fit in the tablecloths that they tied around their waists to make aprons, the silence remained.

What Michael Ruhlman said in his book *The Soul of a Chef* was true. I ate foods that I normally would have gagged on and they tasted great. I probably would have enjoyed the offal menu (I stuck out my tongue when the waiter mentioned it) simply because of the skilled preparation. I repeatedly asked Chris what I was eating; most of my vegetables were unrecognizable. They looked like vegetables I had encountered but tasted a million times better than anything I had ever had. The flavors of each course were carefully balanced, which created a harmony throughout the meal. The quality, seasoning, and texture of each ingredient was unlike anything I know. Each course left me satisfied and filled, the experience lingering in my mouth. It was the most incredible meal of my life, but it wasn't perfect. There were things that I would have changed.

Halfway through the meal I leaned over the table and whispered to Chris, "Can you cook like this?"

"I might be able to if I had the amount of staff they have here, but we wouldn't have a restaurant anymore."

"What do you mean?"

"Excuse me, waiter. I don't think that my butter-poached lobster is cooked all the way through," Chris joked.

I laughed and knew that he was right. The flesh of lobster cooked in butter is translucent and looks underdone.

Keller appeared later on in the shadows of the kitchen door.

"There he is," I whispered with giddy delight.

"Oh, can I touch you?" Chris said sarcastically.

"Yes, but it's going to cost you five dollars. No, wait. Make it ten. I just saw him again."

I would tell you how much the meal for two cost, but my mother would gasp in horror and I would get a twenty-minute lecture from my accountant. On the way back to the hotel, we discussed the meal. My concept of the perfect restaurant was still intact, oddly unaffected by the French Laundry.

I wish I had been more sure of myself when I attended the James Beard Awards a year earlier. I invited Kate to come along when Chris decided at the last minute that he didn't want to go. I figured Kate would be the perfect guest because she's the kind of friend who would hold your hair back from your face while you vomit grapefruit juice through your nose and sob with the agony of kidney pain. (She still won't eat grapefruit.) I was confident she could handle the Beard awards. I'll never forget our third night at college during Labor Day weekend at two A.M. I called meekly from my side of the room, "Kate, will you take me to the hospital?" I had this night in mind when I called last May and asked, "Kate, will you go to the James Beard Awards with me?" As true as always, Kate and I went to battle. I had purchased one ticket for Chris months ago, which I would use, and I got Kate a press pass from a friend. We hopped in the car and drove to the Marriott Marquis in Times Square. Kate and I had been to the Marquis many times before. Chris's older brother, Bernie, used to be the banquet chef there. Bernie would be on hand tonight as a volunteer chef coordinator along with hundreds of other Marriott staff who slip in and out of formal events unnoticed.

Kate and I arrived completely, totally, absolutely without question underdressed for the black-tie affair. We weren't wearing jeans, but we weren't wearing evening gowns, either. The girl checking press passes at an eight-foot banquet table looked skeptical. What newspaper was Kate, aka Lee White, from? Where was the *Norwich Bulletin*? Was she going to write a story about the awards? Did she have a business card? No? What was the fax number of the newspaper? The girl must have finally believed that we were dressed and acting like press, so she let us in.

We had arrived late and weren't sure which room everyone was in or on what floor. A couple hundred people were roaming the hallways smoking. We found our way to the upper balcony and watched about fifteen minutes of cookbook awards. Bored, tired, uncomfortable, overwhelmed, and hungry, we sought the familiar refuge of the rotating restaurant on the top floor. After a sufficient amount of alcohol for Kate, sugar for me, and confidence boosting for both of us, we returned to the banquet floors and found my brother-in-law Bernie. Those paper chef hats always make me laugh. Apparently each of the one hundred folds around the hat represents a different way to cook an egg. Why you would wear that on your head is beyond me. Bernie, complete with hat, clipboard, and groupies, greeted us as cool as possible. He was one of the top chefs in charge of this little (fewer than three thousand people) event. As we stood in the middle of the reception, with twenty-five top Italian chefs serving bite-size portions to hoards of hungry award-goers, it suddenly occurred to me why I was so uncomfortable. The room was mostly filled with restaurant people—chefs, writers, and press—none of whom were used to dressing in tuxedoes. I laughed as I watched men pull at their pants and women teeter on unnaturally high heels. I brought myself back to the conversation with Bernie just in time to hear one of his chefs say, "You're not a real chef anymore when you give up your chef coat for a tuxedo. These are the events that we cater, not the ones that we attend."

Bernie showed me the 150-page folder required to organize the equipment, food, and chefs during the reception. Then he pointed out the famous New York chefs as they strolled by.

"That's Jean-Louis," he said, gesturing.

"Jean-Louis who?" I asked.

"Palladin," he replied, as if no one else on earth had the same first name.

"There's Jean-Georges," he continued.

"George who?" I asked.

"Jean-Georges Vongerichten," he replied.

"Oh," I said. Kate just nodded in agreement. Bernie quickly grew tired of being the tour guide and wandered away to take care of his organizational responsibilities. Kate and I were left on our own. We scoured the room for vegetarian items. We stopped by the Al Forno restaurant table just to say that we had seen the chef/owners, George Germon and Johanne Killeen, even though I don't know them. They were serving something white in a shot glass with caviar on top. The shot glass had their logo on it, and I jokingly told Kate I was going to steal it for Chris. She told me I was being a loser, then dared me to do it. I caved under the peer pressure, rinsed it in the bathroom, wrapped it in some toilet paper, and stuffed it in Kate's purse. With that excitement out of the way, Kate actually ate a ravioli with a whole, uncooked egg yolk swimming in it. I stuck to the water. Mostly we just stood in the center of the room and felt like dorks.

The highlight of the night came after our attempt to conquer the press room. We cautiously opened the door with the paper taped on it. PRESS ONLY, it warned. Once inside we found ourselves in the press hallway. There were many side rooms with interviews, photo shoots, and other important gatherings going on. We quickly turned around, walked out the door, and almost ran into a man. There was a painfully long pause as he tried to figure out how to get around us, and we tried to figure out how to not make asses out of ourselves. Time caught up and we rushed on giggling.

"Oh my God. Do you know who that was?"

"Oh my God, yes. It was Charlie."

"Charlie who?"

"Charlie Trotter!"

It was definitely time to go home. The only chef we had recognized at the Beard awards was one who owned a restaurant, named after him, in Chicago. Neither Kate nor I have been to the Windy City, and we probably wouldn't have recognized him if not for the twenty-five award medallions around his neck.

I was almost as excited when I got to see Tim Mondavi (Robert Mondavi's son) for the first time. It was during the most interesting wine tasting I ever attended, at the Fine Arts Museum in Boston. Tim Mondavi was the speaker. I figured that I could take a nap somewhere in the back of the room without being noticed. The people we went with had other intentions. They sat at the very first table in front of Mondavi. I could have soaked him with my wine if I spilled it just right. Seven glasses sat before me, none of which I was going to drink. All of the cabernets from the 1999 Mondavi collection and a barrel sample (that's rotting grapes that haven't become wine yet) from the 2000 vintage. Mondavi began talking about the wine and the vineyard while I watched the last snow of the season fall in the court-yard through the massive two-story window behind him. I ate some crackers and tried to look attentive. Then in the middle of a long-winded wine sentence, Mondavi said "shit." Right there in a room filled with one hundred wine snobs (or cork dorks, as Jerry likes to call them), seven hundred wineglasses, crackers, linen, water, and spit buckets. I couldn't believe it. Everyone else politely showed no reaction, but I was shocked. I actually listened to what he was saying after that. When he finished talking he asked everyone to taste the wine and tell him what they thought. Tell Tim Mondavi what you think of his wine. Just taste the wines all at once. No long, boring descriptions. No lengthy conversations about dirt. Just drink and enjoy. I was so happy I nearly forgot about how stressed I was. The glasses were huge. I was sitting five feet from Mondavi. He would be able to see that I wasn't drinking his wine. I swirled, sniffed, held the glasses to the light, and traded for Chris's empty glasses. I hope Mondavi didn't notice. He seemed like a pretty cool guy, and I didn't want to insult him after he'd led the least painful tasting I had ever attended.

Chris loves to go to wine tastings almost as much as he loves going to ethnic markets. If he could wear jeans and a T-shirt to wine events, he'd try to go to one every week. I also found out early in our relationship, while we were visiting/torturing Kate in Monterey, California, that he loves to visit aquariums. Kate unwittingly suggested the excursion thinking that it would be a nice touristy activity to occupy us. Restaurant folks can be more than a little annoying when they have too much free time. Little did Kate know what we were in for that day.

Most aquariums are filled with thousands of children milling about while frantic parents attempt to keep track of them in the darkened room. There are two types of children. The first group ("Seen one fish, you've seen 'em all") runs from one viewing glass to the next. They push their way up to the front, peer for a second or two, then move to the next. The second group of children are completely captivated by watching one fish for hours. They wipe their grubby, drool-covered hands (who says I shouldn't have children?) on the glass in an effort to get the fish's attention. They smile, point, and laugh as the fish completes endless doughnuts in the tank.

Chris falls somewhere between the two. He'll run to the glass of the tank, push the children to the side, quickly iden-tify the fish as a wild striped bass, and explain how it should be prepared. Just when the parents are about to turn their heads in disbelief, he runs to the next tank.

"Gross. Sea urchins. I had them once in a sorbet, and it was so disgusting. I don't think that I'll ever eat them again. Look over there. Skate wing! They're excellent sautéed with leeks."

He's easily turned off by the species that can't be eaten, so we finish with our seafood lesson in one third the amount of time that the average family takes. I used to enjoy the peaceful, meditative quality of aquariums. I could stare for hours without banging on the glass or drooling at the dreamlike creatures floating in the clear water. Now I just wonder which plants and animals in the tank can be eaten and at what price. The worst is endangered sea life. This is where Chris becomes like the drooling child. He caresses the tank window and sighs, "Swordfish, so sweet. You can't buy them anymore; they were overfished. Maybe in a few more years."

It is this childlike quality that keeps us going back to Disney World for vacation each year. Chris never tires of the music, the rides, and, of course, the food. Going on vacation seems to be a lot easier for him than it is for me. I should have known that I was in trouble when the clock at our house got stuck at 8:40 just hours before we left for our last "vacation." It should have been a sign, but I was far too stressed to notice. Just twenty-four hours before we left, I checked my business bank account on-line to make sure that we had enough money for payroll, which would come out of the bank while we were away. Much to my dismay, I discovered the money was all gone. How could this be? Had I overpaid the purveyors? Had we not made enough money? I resisted the urge to bash my head on the desk and looked more closely at the account. We had just survived our busiest week ever, thanks to a *New York Times* review, and we had hosted an eighty-dollar-per-person wine dinner on

Thursday. There had to be enough money. As my stomach did Tae Bo, I scanned the computer screen, searching for how I had completely screwed up. Then I paused. The bank had removed five of my payments twice. Only five thousand dollars. Twice. I lifted the phone, punched in numbers, and began to scream. With the money returned to my account, I regained enough sanity to look more closely at it. This is when I noticed the $1,326.89 charge from an on-line computer company. I'm pretty sure that I would have remembered getting a new computer. The one I have now freezes, crashes, plays dead, and is generally a pain in the ass. An hour later, after a dozen phone calls to discover the proper procedure for something of this nature, I sat with the policeman (who had helped me with my illegal payroll-fee withdrawal during the previous year) and filled out another statement. I eventually learned that there was another Courtney Febbroriello (yeah, right) who had received my computer in New Rochelle, New York. I also learned that the bank card with the Visa symbol on it doesn't mean that I am protected from fraud. And I only had six more hours until I was supposed to leave on "vacation." I still needed to enter sales in my old computer, finish payroll, do a schedule for Metro Express, talk to Jerry about hiring dishwashers, go over the caterings with the sous-chef, review the procedure for Thanksgiving-to-Go orders, pack some clothing, and find that guy I was going on "vacation" with. I say "vacation" because work never ends. Where there is food, there is work. On the plane at seven A.M. I slept. When we checked into our hotel, the room wasn't ready yet. I slept on the beach. When I woke up, I finished and faxed the payroll. I ordered balloons and flowers for a friend who would be celebrating a birthday at our restaurant while we were away. I ordered a fax machine cartridge for delivery to Metro Express with a secured credit card and went back to sleep. When I woke up, we were supposed to be on vacation, but the Food & Wine festival at Epcot was in its final week. Frederick Ek, the exclusive importer of E. Guigal wines, was on premise. We started by attending his advanced wine seminar, then we enjoyed his reserve dinner of foie gras and French wines, and finished with an informal cocktail party where his wines were poured. Chris had a great time, and I learned quite a bit about the whole experience of attending a wine event rather than hosting one.

The most painful part of the week was attending a cooking demonstration by one of *Food & Wine* magazine's top ten new chefs. The chef was completely unprepared for the demonstration and didn't have much skill in the kitchen. Chris was convinced that she had forgotten to pack salt. Even as I offered a million excuses as to why the chef was unprepared and why the food might not have been up to expectations, Chris moaned and groaned his way around the world showcase. What was it that we were doing wrong? Why didn't we have the right connections? What would it take to get to the top? As we walked at breakneck speed past

France, it occurred to me that we were supposed to be on vacation. I'm sure that most people don't try to infiltrate the Food & Wine festival while at Disney World. They probably wander mindlessly around the park while nibbling on chocolate-covered mouse ears.

When we got home the clock was still stuck on 8:40, the second hand beating endlessly in the same place. A week had passed since we had last been in the restaurant.

STALKING RESTAURANT REVIEWERS, AVOIDING FOODIES, TREATING CHEF ENVY

*S*ince work doesn't ever stop when we are on vacation, we always come back to the restaurant with more ideas about how to improve our business and reputation. One of the ways to increase the visibility of the restaurant is to get reviewed, but reviewing can be tricky. Most restaurateurs loathe food critics. They fear the impact a review can have on their business and are the first to tell you that critics have no idea what they are eating. I don't think a review can ruin a good restaurant and critics are supposed to represent the average diner. I do wish that the general population understood reviews better. A review is one person's opinion of the restaurant during one or two meals.

A reviewer is like any other person who dines out. Perhaps he and his wife disagreed on the car ride over, or they drove an hour and a half in traffic to get to the restaurant. Maybe his mother-in-law loves the place, and the reviewer would rather suffer water torture before admitting that she might be right about anything. One Connecticut reviewer unknowingly visited a neighborhood café that was BYOB. She arrived for dinner after the state-mandated nightly closing of the liquor stores and was unable to buy a bottle of wine. The first paragraph and a half of her review lamented her dry situation, and she was clearly embarrassed to be unprepared in front of her friends. She even wrote that she and her guests would have rather stayed home and eaten omelettes than dined in this particular establishment. The restaurant got a bad review just because they didn't tell the reviewer that they were BYOB when she made the reservation.

Sometimes reviews are politically motivated. The owner of the paper or an editor has a close friend who owns a restaurant. Or the restaurant spends a lot of money on advertising. When a reviewer finds a piece of glass in her salad and the restaurant still manages a three-star review, something is clearly amiss. Most reviewers don't make much money, and the newspaper might give them the opportunity to dine at a restaurant only once. Better hope it's not on the night when the chef walks out because he is hung over and resentful because the owner just explained why he can't call a waitress a cunt. (Not that it matters to reviewers or customers, since there are no "preview prices"; dinner should be as close to perfect every night.)

One local reviewer was fired because she didn't actually

go to the place that she reviewed. She took the word of a friend who told her that the restaurant was mediocre and that the clam chowder was particularly bad. The reviewer might have gotten away with it, but the restaurant owner called the paper and said in no uncertain terms that he would never serve clam chowder. He was allergic to clams.

There is a group that most legitimate reviewers belong to called the Association of Food Journalists. This association was formed in 1974 after a U.S. senator called food writers "the whores of journalism" during a food editors' conference. The AFJ has a code of ethics that everyone in the organization is supposed to follow: Rules like eating at a restaurant more than once, being anonymous, and not accepting anything for free are very important to them.

The critics for most large newspapers follow the ethics closely, but there are always exceptions. In one large city most of the restaurant owners not only know what a certain reviewer looks like, but they have gone to great lengths to discover his likes and dislikes. It is very difficult for a critic to maintain his anonymity when he has been reviewing for a while and making public appearances during book signings. According to a local magazine that wrote a piece on the food reviewer in this city, most of the restaurants that received four stars last year featured goat cheese appetizers. He must like goat cheese! Quick, everyone come up with a new dish.

But I'm glad that there is a group like the Association of Food Journalists. I think that the reviewers who follow the ethics should have a little "AFJ" after their names. It would help their readers immensely. Most readers would be surprised to know that the *Farmington Valley Post* "reviewer" tells you when she's coming, identifies herself at the door, and asks you to pick up her bill. She's a very friendly woman, but her readers have a right to know that she is not having the same experience they would have. The *Hartford Advocate* doesn't tell restaurants when they are coming, but they trade advertising for gift certificates if they are planning on reviewing. Just write "Please present this gift certificate to your server at the beginning of your meal" and the restaurant can easily identify the critic. Reviewers are supposed to be anonymous so they will have the same experience as the reader. The public should know when the review has been compromised.

No matter how legitimate reviewers are, they all seem to be upset about star, spoon, and diamond systems. It is difficult to dole out stars to completely different styles of restaurants. A fine-dining establishment that forgot to replace the silverware after each course, charred a rare steak, never filled water glasses, and confused the order might win a two-star review. The hottest pizza place in town might have crispy crust, creative toppings, hearty lasagne, and earn two stars. Who could possibly make sense of such a system? Most of the time the reader only sees the stars and doesn't remember the review at all.

But this isn't the hardest part of the job. The most painful part is when a disgruntled restaurant owner writes threatening letters, faithful customers leave nasty voice mail, and your e-mail box is filled with messages on how much you suck. You couldn't pay me enough for that job. (I also couldn't deal with food poisoning on a regular basis. Tom Sietsema of the *Washington Post* says that he eats bad food so his readers don't have to.)

Food critics take reviews as personally as restaurant owners. No one enjoys hate mail. Reviewers are always accused of closing restaurants and they worry about this "power." If a restaurant is going down, a bad review just speeds up the process. That critic who was upset about her dry dinner at the neighborhood café? We went to the restaurant a week later and couldn't get in the place. A review can kill a restaurant less than a year old, but an established one that has a following will keep on going—at least in Connecticut.

The reverse is also true: A great review in the first six months can doom a restaurant. The diners' expectations are too high, and the restaurant isn't prepared to handle the demand. Customers are quickly disappointed and never return.

I think that reviewing should be done by a group like it is in Europe. Those *Michelin* guides seem to provide the closest thing to an impartial rating. The *Zagat* guide is not the same, believe me. The guide isn't always accurate because only a few people in Connecticut sort through all of the comments and decide which ones to include, unlike in New York City, where a group makes the decisions. According to the *Zagat* guide, the estimated cost for dinner at Metro Bis went from twenty-eight dollars per person in 2000 to forty-one dollars in the 2001/2002 guide without our having changed our prices at all. The *Zagat* guide, however, is the best worldwide reviewing tool that we have. I have one from just about every place I've ever visited. I can't stand going somewhere new and not having the guide. It may not always be right, but it's usually pretty close.

I try to fill out a *Zagat* survey every year. Me, a restaurant owner. I am not alone. There is no way to filter out restaurant owners and their friends from the survey results. The people who fill out the survey also don't have to send in receipts to prove that they actually went to each of the restaurants they comment on. This allows restaurateurs to easily influence the guide.

No publication is immune. Who are the readers of *Connecticut Magazine* during August, restaurant-poll month? More likely than not, they are restaurateurs and their friends. The magazines aren't naive. One of their advertising salesmen told me that they produce 30 percent more magazines for that voting month. Americans don't run to the polls for elections, so why would they run to the grocery store, buy a magazine, and vote for their favorite restaurant? Winning a readers' poll carries a lot more weight than buying an ad. The money spent on the magazines is a very worthwhile investment.

Despite all of this, the public still puts its faith in the opinion of one reviewer on one given night, and restaurants are still willing to go to enormous lengths to flush the critics out. Certain restaurants have resorted to having lists of reviewers' phone numbers and using caller ID. Some hire waitstaff who can identify the critics. Still others have pictures of reviewers in wait stations or on the kitchen walls. One such place posts a caption underneath the photo that reads, "She could mean your job." My favorite hunting rumor is about a restaurant in New York that supposedly hired a private investigator to get a picture of the reviewer.

Reviewers sense this fox hunt and have friends make reservations, dress in disguise, use their wives' maiden names, or bring other people's children to dinner. Discovery can mean their jobs, so the game continues. Some reviewers are angered by restaurateurs attempting to discover them because they think it's cheating.

Chris met the restaurant reviewer of the *Hartford Courant* by accident. Chris was calling me from a pay phone out of state when I heard a man on the phone next to him. "Hi, this is Bill Daley. I'd like to check my messages." I gasped. Chris nearly dropped the phone while he stared at the unearthed reviewer. He didn't resent Bill despite the way he had torn apart our crème brûlée and scoffed at our New York strip steak with crispy onions. Some chefs hold grudges for years, like the chef in the play *Fully Committed* who blows off a writer from *Gourmet* magazine after she insults one of his dishes.

Chris was more fascinated than resentful. A chef seeing a restaurant reviewer is like a single woman seeing a flasher on the street. There's shock and bewilderment. Bill immediately sensed that he had been discovered and gave himself up. Every time Chris sees another chef, he is forced to give some sort of description of Bill since all restaurants are supposed to band together against the evil reviewers. Chris has portrayed him variously as a short, wide, bald man and a tall, hairy, bearded man. Each time someone asks, we change Bill's appearance to amuse ourselves. Restaurant owners go out of their way to meet, write, or call us, hoping to get the inside line on Bill. It's really not that hard to get reviewed. One just sends a menu to the paper and waits. That's all we did.

Our first reviews saved us. We did not change the name of the restaurant for fear of too big an opening with hoards of customers standing in the entryway. We were worried about making a bad first impression, which turned out not to be a problem because no one noticed we were under new ownership. We struggled from bill to bill, customer to customer, until the first review.

Before that review I sensed impending doom at each table. I eyed each customer nervously and watched each ticket coming into the kitchen. I prayed on the not-so-smooth days that no restaurant reviewers were present.

Whenever four different appetizers and entrées were ordered on the same table, panic caused me to race across the dining room to check on the table that might be critiquing our food and service.

Our first reviewer came on a Tuesday night from the *Hartford Advocate*, an alternative weekly paper. It was just two women, not a table of four. They came only that one Tuesday. I realized that we were being reviewed after they had left. The women had paid with the hundred-dollar gift certificate that I had traded for advertising no less than a week earlier. I pumped the waitress for more information. What had they eaten? Did they seem happy? Did they say anything about the food? We held our breath, crossed our fingers, and waited. Two weeks later our first review was printed with four stars. She loved everything from the curtains to the dessert. Wonderful? Fabulous? Who could ask for anything more? Chris was devastated. The only mention of the chef/owner was: "Courtney Febbroriello, late of the celebrated West Street Grill in Litchfield, has an appreciation of the truly different coupled with a sly, intelligent sense of fun." I can't believe the reviewer got all of that from watching me walk through the dining room a couple times. Here, at last, was a perk for being wife. The staff however, enjoyed commenting on my "sly, intelligent sense of fun" while I carefully dumped ravioli for my lunch into a pot of boiling water and stared at it until it was done.

Really the only problem with the review was that my

name was used instead of Chris's. He wasn't listed anywhere. His first independent review, and I got all of the credit. Had I known how quickly I would fade into anonymity, I would have gloated for a few more hours, but Chris was so upset that I felt bad. The last place that he worked never gave him credit. He was finally out on his own, and he still went unnoticed. I got a framed corrected copy of the review from our ad agent, but Chris wasn't fully recovered until after the next three reviews. My father, however, was delighted. He still sends copies of the review, with our last name highlighted, along with his business correspondence to people in the area.

The next review was from the *Hartford Courant*, and it knocked us over. It came out on a Sunday. On Monday the worst waitress on earth and I did sixty-nine lunches in an hour and a half in our sixty-four-seat restaurant. Before the review came out, we usually had ten to fifteen people for lunch. I should have had four people on that day. It was the most horrendous shift of my life. I remember running back to the kitchen at the brink of lunch's disaster and telling Chris that we weren't going to make it. We couldn't handle it. We were going to die. I don't think he took me seriously until I started dumping dirty dishes in the bread station because there wasn't enough time to take five more steps to the dishwasher around the corner. I'm not exactly sure what the worst waitress on earth was doing. I didn't have time to look. This was the last time that I have truly behaved badly at a table. I actually asked one party, "Would you like dessert, or do you just want to leave?"

I was sure that the two women on the banquette had been waiting for decades for dessert menus or a check. They looked at me blankly and told me that they were all set.

The dishwasher quit that day, too. He was an old raisin of an alcoholic. The poison had ravaged his body and taken his driver's license, so he walked to work with a brown paper bag. Usually, by the time lunch was half over, he had the shakes and was sweating like I never thought possible. Boy, did he smell. Then he seemed to have discovered the generic vodka that was used for the vodka cream sauce on a lunch pasta. Chris and Al watched the vodka disappear while the pasta stayed in the fridge and eventually realized that the dishwasher wasn't shaking around one-thirty like he normally did. On this fateful day, they poured white vinegar into an empty vodka bottle and hid the real stuff. At the end of that shift, dishes stacked to the ceiling, the dishwasher left with his breath smelling of vinegar. We shrugged and rushed to keep up with the new business.

After we survived the first reviews and the early years in the restaurant, we started to ask each other, "What's next?" The answer was the James Beard House. James Beard is considered the father of American cooking and was the author of many books. After his death in 1985, his close friend Julia Child thought his memory would be best honored if his home was converted into a pseudo-restaurant.

This way James Beard's spirit would remain at the forefront of American cooking. Peter Kump organized the effort and the James Beard Foundation was created. Chefs come from all over the country to cook at the James Beard House in Greenwich Village. With approximately 350 meals served a year and, it is said, more than 5,000 chefs trying to get in, it is considered an honor to be invited to cook at the Beard House.

Chris had cooked there a couple years earlier in a Connecticut chefs series dinner with three other chefs. I didn't get to go because there was no room for me in the kitchen, and I wasn't about to eat anything on the menu. Everyone at the communal table would have known I was the chef's fiancée and I wasn't eating any of his food. It would have looked bad. So my parents went instead and seemed to have a great time. My mother in particular enjoyed herself so much that when she went to the bathroom in the middle of dinner, she forgot that the bathroom door was a pocket door and couldn't get out. She banged on the door until Chris's brother Bernie slid the door back into the wall. She was completely embarrassed, but free.

Eager to get a look at the bathroom near the kitchen where my mother had been mortified, I set out to find a way for Chris to do a solo dinner at the Beard House. There are a number of ways to get in. The food media can write letters of recommendation, a famous chef can make a phone call, or a vineyard might host a winemaker's dinner and request a specific chef. We chose the third option since the Northeast representative for Robert Mondavi wines is a good friend. He contacted the representative from New York and spoke with someone at the Beard House. She told him to have us send a press packet and a proposed menu. I did and nothing happened. So a chef friend who had cooked at the house before called to recommend Chris. Bernie put in a good word through the staff that organized the awards dinner. A friend from Les Dames d'Escoffier (a very active and prominent women's culinary group) put in a recommendation as well. Chris called the Beard House and asked if there was a date for the winemaker's dinner. The woman said, "Just because you mail in a press packet doesn't mean that you get to do a dinner." She also said there were many Connecticut chefs trying to cook at the Beard House. Her favorite Connecticut chef was from Greenwich, and he took her to his house in France every year. Somewhat discouraged, we discussed the problems we were having with our Mondavi representative, and he managed to finally get us in.

The Beard House is a really great concept. New Yorkers have the opportunity to enjoy food from around the country without having to leave the city. Diners get to experience culinary trends firsthand in the comfort of their own backyard. Some of the nation's best chefs have showcased their talents in the Beard House, and it has promoted areas in the United States that would have never been associated with great food. The Beard House truly represents American cuisine, but it shouldn't be harder to get into than Guantanamo.

And here's the thing: Chefs selected to cook at the Beard House pay for that honor. All of the food and labor is donated by the chef's restaurant, and often the wine is, too. This can be an enormous expense if the chef and his staff and food must be flown in from, say, Seattle. (Not to mention that the staff traveling with him must be paid and put up somewhere.) We are close by, the wine was donated, and Chris's brother gathered a group of volunteer chefs, so the dinner cost us only a couple thousand dollars.

This money is used by the foundation to fund a multitude of culinary scholarships, maintain the house, preserve the Beard library, and organize the archives. The Beard Foundation also publishes several guides listing the top restaurants, chefs, journalists, food writers, and authors in the country. There is no other center for culinary exploration in the United States where the public can interact so freely with chefs and members of the press.

The house is pretty small, so the expenses aren't too high for food. Chris's dinner sold out with one hundred people who were packed into every inch of available space. I got to see the bathroom downstairs where my mother got stuck and the one upstairs filled with so many mirrors that I got sick looking at myself. I didn't sit at a table, so I was able to roam through the dining room and the kitchen. Bernie had assembled a great Marriott crew, and it was like a reunion for them. It also was one of the easiest dinners they had ever done since most of them had worked with Bernie in Marriott banquet kitchens. They could have easily served one hundred guests while sleeping behind the line. Needless to say, everything went very smoothly as the chefs slid each plate down the counter in assembly-line fashion (there are actual conveyor belts in the Marriott Marquis kitchen). Chris stood at the end of the line, inspected each plate, and handed it to a waiter. During the plating of the third course, after the chefs had consumed six bottles of wine among the ten of them, there was a long discussion about an S&M club called the Vault. When they started talking about a guy who had been almost completely covered in plastic wrap, I decided it might be a good time to go upstairs and mingle with the guests. I could hear Chris and Bernie laughing from the second floor.

Just because a chef cooks at the Beard House doesn't mean that he has achieved national fame, but it does feed his ego a bit. Everyone has heard about the outlandish egos of chefs filled with their own greatness and completely incapable of making any mistakes. Like one chef down south who kicked out customers who asked for salt and pepper. According to the chef, his food was seasoned perfectly and anyone asking for these staples was being insulting. I used to think these chefs were just self-centered jerks who were struggling for respect and recognition until I discovered the phenomena of chef envy. The typical sufferer of chef envy is a home cook who loves food, hates his job, and wishes he had gone to culinary school instead of listening to his parents. It's too late now. He is a doctor, has kids, has a knee problem, but if he had time or if life had been different, he would be just as good as the best chefs in the country. Besides, it isn't that hard to cook. People with chef envy throw dinner parties all the time.

Chef envy manifests itself in a number of ways, which is why it can be tricky to diagnose. Sometimes a person with CE is bitter and feels threatened by a chef. Take, for example, the host at a dinner party who refused to ask for help with his beef tenderloin. Four hours later all the guests were starving and dinner still wasn't ready. Or the woman who marched into the kitchen to tell Chris he had no business owning a restaurant because he did not use celery in his mussel broth. Or a journalist acquaintance at our table at dinner last month who was asked by a waiter if he was ready to order. "Why don't you ask him? He's the chef!" the journalist responded, sneering at the waiter while he gestured to Chris. Just because he's a chef doesn't mean that Chris will know what to order first. Most of the time he's dead silent for the first twenty minutes at a table while he reads the menu and wine list word for word.

CE can also be more subtle. Chris and I attended a fundraising event where a well-known chef was greeting guests with his wife. A woman with CE ran over to the chef, pushed his wife out of the way, and stood with her back toward her while she gushed all over the chef. Another woman with CE burst into our kitchen during our first month of business and insisted that Chris divulge the secret of his chicken gumbo to her. When innocent people suffer from CE, they tend to flock together and call themselves foodies. They are suffering from a serious affliction that can cause them to trail chefs in a desperate attempt to gain their attention. "I loved your tuna special tonight. Can I work in your kitchen? Can we go out to dinner? Can I have your children? Can I spend every second of the rest of my life with you? Please?" And this is why chefs suffer from over-inflated egos. CE has created a codependency that can be eliminated only with intensive therapy.

When Chris walks into the dining room, people watch and whisper to one another in agreement that he is the chef. They talk loudly about how great the scallops are in an effort to get his attention. He doesn't even notice. He's on his way to the bar to get some more club soda. Chris will stop at a table and chat about the truffle oil on the pasta tonight. I was just at the same table no more than ten minutes ago, and they argued with me about whether or not the truffle oil was from black or white truffles. Even though I insisted that the oil is from white truffles, they didn't believe me. But they absorb the chef's words—much as dried mushrooms are revitalized by warm water. The guests smile and laugh and act as if the holy grace of a culinary god has descended upon them. Chris, as always oblivious, returns to the kitchen to put up a few more tables. I just want to scream, "If it wasn't for me, you wouldn't have any truffle oil. First of all, the chef would have no clean clothing to leave the house in. Just ask him about his light-versus-heavy separation of the laundry rather than the more conventional light versus dark. I can't tell you how many pieces of clothing he has ruined. And let's not even talk about the bleach incidents. Believe me, without clean clothes you wouldn't want him to leave the kitchen. Second, I paid the bill for that truffle oil. If the almighty chef was responsible for the bill, it could have ended up anywhere. Third, these people wouldn't be dining here tonight if they hadn't seen Chris on the news last week. Who contacted the station and dragged the chef out of bed at six o'clock on a Sunday morning?" Yes, the wife.

It's not that I don't think Chris is a great chef. As far as I can tell without really eating any of his food, he is. But he is no demigod, that's for sure. And is any chef?

Chris is always surrounded by foodies with some degree of CE. On those rare occasions when he does go to the grocery store, women follow him around to see what is in his basket. And everyone whom Chris encounters wants to tell him what they ate the night before and how it was prepared. "I had the best pork chops last night. My wife seasoned them with peppermint, braised them in the oven for three hours, and served them with mustard-covered Brussels sprouts. You should have that on the menu."

Foodies—the ones with more food knowledge—love to argue about the best way to roast a chicken or make demiglaze. CE can cause a food journalist to launch a spontaneous culinary Trivial Pursuit contest in order to prove that he knows more about Chinese food history than the so-called chef. There is always a discussion about the ultimate barbecue or the nuances of smoking. Chris comfortably joins in any conversation whenever the topic is food.

His favorite foodies are foragers. These people, who constitute a strange subculture of the foodie world, are usually unpretentious, solitary folks who spend a lot of time in the woods. We have a mycologist who hunts for mushrooms and fiddlehead ferns. Nothing is more amusing than watching her come through the kitchen door. Chris will literally run off of the line in the middle of service to greet her and examine the contents of her basket.

"This oyster mushroom is unbelievable," he'll sigh.

Then they chat in the corner about the different ways to prepare the woodsy catch and how the weather conditions are affecting the spores. In exchange for the freshest of mushrooms, the mycologist will come for dinner with her husband. Chris will prepare one dish from her supply and let her choose the rest of her meal from the menu. Sometimes I stop by the table and pretend to be interested in the conversation.

At least the mycologist isn't mean like other foodies tend

to be. In most food discussions I try to stay awake and hide my vegetarianism for as long as possible. Most foodies take vegetarianism as a personal attack, as if I peed all over their BMW on my way to their party. Clearly I am ridiculous, immature, and uncultured because I don't eat meat. Normally a long discussion ensues about how wrong and unfulfilled my pitiful meatless life is. Actually I'm glad that I don't eat meat when I am with this type of person. I don't like to be competitive and it is easier to feign ignorance. I never liked the flavors of most fishes, for example. Instead of having an excuse like vegetarianism, I would have to explain to the foodie who is in rapture over sea bass why I have no taste, which would probably be harder.

I recently read about a woman who quit being a vegetarian after fifteen years (though she probably wasn't really a vegetarian since she allowed crunchy, smoky pancetta in her diet). She said that she had been selfish as a vegetarian because friends felt compelled to prepare more challenging dinners when she was invited to dinner. This had never occurred to me. Chris said that it was no big deal. Our friends are much more stressed about cooking for him, and not everyone uses meat in every single side dish. It's unbelievable that anyone would want to attempt to feed both of us.

Chris always says, "It's just food. Look where it ends up twenty-four hours after you eat it. You just can't take it that seriously."

4

DINNER

THE BATTLE OF
THE BISTRO

To the couple I just sat on table one it isn't just about food. It's about their anniversary, or a birthday, or a night when they don't have to cook. It doesn't matter what the reviews said. It doesn't matter that Chris cooked in the Beard House. What matters is that they have a good experience regardless of what is happening behind the scenes.

Tonight everything is going well. The dishwasher has been fixed in time for dinner; all of the staff is present and ready for work. I was not so lucky one night when Chris was cooking at a charity function. It usually isn't a problem when he leaves, but this time there was no dishwasher and one of the waiters didn't show up. I ran back and forth across the dining room picking up dishes, hostessing, and chatting with the tables that I knew. Then I ran back into the bowels of the kitchen and scraped dishes, tried not to sear my hands on the 180-degree plates, and made sure that I stayed clean and pretty. (Well, at least clean.) Then I grabbed a paper towel, wiped the kitchen film off my face, cut three baskets of bread, and made a dash for the door.

On my way past a table a gentleman hailed me. For what? More water? Butter for the bread? Cook his steak more? No. He wanted to know if the St. Christopher's medallion around my neck was an Olympic medal. I smiled briefly or maybe not at all and quipped that I had won the gold for sprinting. Then I dashed toward the front door after hurtling over the waitstaff in my path. I wished that I could have just shot-put the nine people lingering in the entryway into their chairs, but none of the tables was set from the first seating yet.

"It will just be a couple of minutes while I reset your tables," I chirp.

Back to the kitchen. No clean silverware. I run it through the dishwasher, gather the other items for the tables, and complete my race through the dining room. As I'm scrubbing the pots at the end of the night in swill up to my elbows, all I can think about is how much fun it must be to be the wife of the chef.

The wife of the chef must spend her morning at the gym with her personal trainer. (This is her secret to staying so thin.) After her workout she has her hair and nails done and gets a rejuvenating massage. Then she dresses for work and runs a few business errands. She arrives at the restaurant just prior to dinner and enjoys a nine-course tasting menu prepared personally by her husband the chef. The she mills around the dining room greeting customers, kissing, shaking hands, and expounding on the specials that she enjoyed earlier. At the end of the long day, say eight o'clock, she heads back home and relaxes while watching the Food Network and resting her feet in warm herbal water. Her chef husband arrives at home soon after with dessert course in hand, and they live happily ever after.

Tonight I'm closer to that myth. I'm hostessing, and dinner is starting to pick up. Service at night is much more intricate. There are dinner drinks, wine service, appetizers, soup spoons, crumbing, cappuccino, and many more steps. I help with some of that, but my job is mostly to watch the door. Listen, hostessing is a challenging profession that is completely unappreciated.

To some people where they sit is much more important than what they eat. Customers will swarm to a restaurant with a patio overlooking a lake and dine on food that should have died in the sixties and have a wonderful time. If hostesses had more of an impact on restaurant design, the world would be a better place; at least mine would be. No one wants to sit by the door or the bathroom. Some people want to be by the kitchen; others consider it the worst table in the house. Some like to be by the wall; others want to have lots of space. Some want to be in the middle of the room; others want a dark little corner. The perfect table to one person is an insult to another.

I know that our dining room isn't perfect. There are many design flaws that I will improve on when I have money, but I am surprised by restaurants that have been in business for more than ten years and still have "bad" tables. I am shocked by the ones that spend tens of thousands for restaurant designers who create gorgeous dining rooms with uncomfortable spaces. I often read about restaurants that save a few tables each night for celebrities who might drop in. Those tables are in the best places so that these special guests are as comfortable as possible. I don't know any famous people personally, and I couldn't identify them, either. But I've never told a table eating dessert that they have to leave because the governor just walked in. I hope that I can rearrange the dining room so that everyone can feel like a celebrity and everyone is at the best table. I don't want to have to think about whether or not a couple will put up a fight when I try to seat them on table eight. I want them to be happy no matter where they are seated.

Unfortunately, this is not the case tonight. I have already seated half of the dining room when two people enter the restaurant.

"Good evening," I say, smiling.

"Hello. Cathy, where do you want to sit? I'd prefer to be along the wall."

I ignore their conversation and take them to table eleven. It's not along the wall. The only tables I have along the wall are for parties of four. Seating people is a power issue for some reason. I try to do the best that I can for each group. I seat the tables along the wall first, and then I seat according to reservation. If you made your reservation an hour before service, then you will probably be in the middle of the room.

When this couple gave me their name, I glanced at the book and saw that their reservation had a phone number next to it, which means that they made the reservation during the day. When I lead them to the middle of the room, Cathy makes a face, looks uncomfortable, and lets him know that she does not like the table. They stand next to the table. I put down the menus hoping that they will take the hint and sit. The man starts to look around the room.

"Can we have that table?"

"I'm sorry, sir, that table is for four people."

"What about that one?"

"That reservation was made for an anniversary two months ago."

"They're not here. Why can't we have that table?"

"We seat our tables according to when the reservations come in. The earlier reservations are seated along the wall."

"So this is the only table that we can have?"

"The one behind you is also available."

"That one isn't any good, either."

"I'm sorry, sir."

At this point the couple must make a decision. It's the male ego versus the need to eat. Sometimes the couple storms out, sometimes they stay and pout, sometimes they relax and have a good time. It's up to them. If they leave because they don't like the table, I feel bad, but there's not too much that I can do. I would be more than a little irritated if I made a reservation two months ago and some jerk who is trying to get laid took my table. Sometimes a long-term reservation gets stuck in the middle, but I always try to get them along the wall. We only have sixty-four seats, and maneuvering the room on a Saturday night can be difficult.

Cathy decides to stay, and I tell the waiter to get to the table fast. After all of the six-thirty seating is in, I have a couple of minutes between the next set of reservations and the running of the food. I take a brisk walk through the dining room. I just sat table eleven, seventeen, six, and seven. They all need bread and most of the waitstaff is at the bar mixing drinks. Jerry is running food to table three. On the way by he says, "Did you see the hair on table five? She looks like Barbarella."

I get in a quick "Who's Barbarella?" before Jerry crosses into the dining room. Then I cut four baskets of bread and load four ramekins with hummus. On my way into the dining room, Jerry is on his way back into the kitchen to run desserts.

"She was in a space movie in the seventies. She had this funky do like in *Austin Powers*," he says as he whisks by.

I drop all of my bread baskets at the appropriate tables and head back to the kitchen. Jerry is about to run the apps to table two.

"She's got some crazy hair out there on five," I say.

"Did you see it?" he laughs. "It probably took her three hours to get it up like that."

"It's probably a wig," I joke to his back as he makes his way to the dining room again.

I grab the entrées on table ten and walk back through the dining room. The front door is crammed with a six top that I don't have a table for yet. I greet them and let them know that I'll have a table soon. I find the waiter for tables fifteen and sixteen. One is on dessert and the other has been sitting with the bill for a long time.

"I need them now. That's the six top at the door," I plead while I gather their table settings. When I head to the bar to get their glasses, the host of the six top glares at me.

"I had a seven-thirty res-er-va-tion," he hisses.

"I'll have a table for you in a couple of minutes, sir," I reply. They just walked in three minutes ago at 7:43. I marked the time down in the reservation book. When I look up from the book, he's glaring at me, so I head back to the kitchen as both tables that he is waiting for get up. As I reset the tables, I hear a wineglass being tipped over on the other side of the room. I rush over with a napkin to wipe the floor. I clear the appetizers that are floating in wine and order new ones from the kitchen. I replace the paper on top of the table, the tablecloth, and all of the silverware. Then I seat the guy waiting at the door for the six top.

"This is the only table that you have available?" he sneers.

"Yes, sir."

"I wanted something along the windows." He pouts.

"This is all that I have, sir," I reply.

"Well, I guess I'll just have to sit here."

"Uh-huh," I say while I hand him a menu.

The rest of his guests are dead silent. I have the feeling that they don't want to be at the table any more than I do. Thankfully, I'm just a lowly hostess, but I have the ability to walk away from the table. We're in the middle of service, and I still have a lot of table setting and food running to do.

"Watch out for table sixteen," I say to the waiter on my way to clear table four.

COMBAT SKILLS

*A*s I headed back to the dishwashing station loaded down with entrée plates from table four, I thought about the guy on sixteen and my brother. My brother and I obviously come from similar backgrounds. We both spent most of our education in expensive private schools, where most students go on to be doctors and businessmen. Jared was in between his junior and senior year at Gettysburg College last summer when we had one of our famous disagreements, the kind we used to have when our parents would stop the car and pull us apart. We have always fought. I never wanted him in my room, so he would plot ways to infiltrate the premises. He would throw water balloons at my friends and listen in on my phone conversations. He is the quintessential younger brother. We've gotten older, we get along better, but he can still infuriate me with words that make my blood surge through my veins and cause my arms to twitch. Last summer Jared was discussing his plan to become an international attorney. He wanted to be "a player on the world stage." He wanted to be well known, successful, professional, wealthy, powerful, and not like me.

"What's wrong with me?" I demanded.

"Well, nothing really. It's just that you serve the kind of people I want to become. You aren't on the same level. You work for them. You're a servant."

I resisted an intense urge to put him in a choke hold and take him down. (Nothing's worse than the day that you realize that your younger brother is bigger and stronger than you. It happened many years ago, and I don't have a chance at even touching him now.) As the anger boiled, I replied as calmly as possible, "I'm sorry that owning my own business before the age of twenty-five isn't good enough for you."

In the end I was more hurt than angry. It's hard enough to get respect from society when you're in the restaurant business. But my own brother! I would have thought I had a better chance there. He had a point, though. Restaurant workers aren't well respected. To many it is a profession relegated to those who can't make it in the "real" world. A place for misfits and high-school dropouts. But anyone who has worked in the industry knows this simply isn't true.

Being a waiter is not easy. For some reason, everyone thinks that they can do it because they waited on tables in college or had a friend who worked in the food business. (One third of the U.S. population has worked in the restaurant industry.) "What's the big deal?" they say. You take the order, get the food, and bring it to the table. At a casual-dining chain restaurant you might be able to get away with that, but you can't in mine.

First and foremost, the waitstaff must have good personalities or at least be able to fake them well. Then they need to become pseudo-psychologists. They have to examine the needs of each table carefully. Do the guests want to be left alone? Do they want to joke with the waitstaff? Are they in a rush? Waitstaff must also have the knowledge. They need to know what roasted, pan-seared, and all that terminology means. They need to taste the nightly specials and be able to describe unusual ingredients with a friendly authority that puts the guest at ease. They need to know where each ingredient in each special entrée comes from and how each part of the dish is prepared. For example, the soft-shell crabs are from Maryland, lightly floured, and pan-seared. Once the waitstaff have a full education on the specials, they need to combine their personalities and individual styles with their ability to read the guest and make appropriate suggestions for both food and beverages.

After taking a dinner order, the waitstaff in my restaurant mix all of the drinks for their tables and recommend wine to be paired with each dish. The waitstaff are also in control of the timing of the meal. They clear the plates, determine the pace of the guest, and request the next course from the kitchen. Waitstaff need to be able to move quickly and work hard. And they need to organize their time very, very well. There can be no wasted trips.

Waiting on tables professionally requires constant multitasking. Making all of the food for a table come up at the same time in the kitchen can be challenging, but it is much harder to remember the order taken off of table one while making the drinks for table two. Table three just asked for more cream to go with their coffee, and table four needs silverware (this is called being marked) because their appetizers are waiting in the kitchen. Table five just got up and asked for the check because they are trying to make it to an eight o'clock movie but forgot to mention it when they sat down. And the phone won't stop ringing.

It's not that different from the coordination required in the kitchen, but for a waiter everything is really far away. In the kitchen the chef should be able to turn 360 degrees and reach all of the ingredients he needs. This is called his mise en place, or "everything in its place." It means the chef is prepared for service and all the components of each menu item are easily accessible. The waiter, on the other hand, needs to schlep from the bar to the computer to the coffee station to the kitchen to the table. It takes twice as long to complete all of the tasks because all of his service components—his mise en place—are all over the restaurant. In the meantime he can't forget about anything he needs along the way or else he'll have wasted steps. If he goes to the bar to make a drink and passes the computer, he should grab the check for another table while he's there or else he'll have to walk all the way back from the table for which he made the drink to get it later.

The National Restaurant Association is attempting to change the public's perception of waitstaff and other restaurant workers by confronting negative images. They tried to get rid of the GEICO commercial with the waitress who wipes the mayonnaise on the edge of the table when the customer tells her he ordered his sandwich without mayo. GEICO didn't pull the commercial, but Hallmark pulled a card that read, "What's worse than having a group of waiters sing you Happy Birthday? Being one of those waiters."

Great waiters whose work in restaurants is their sole form of income do well financially. A Saturday-night shift of five to six hours can bring in $150 to $250, depending on the night. That's over thirty dollars an hour. A Tuesday lunch shift might bring in only thirty dollars. Most restaurants pay their waitstaff below minimum wage. They earn a standard "waiter's wage," which in Connecticut, is currently $4.74, or $1.96 below minimum wage, and their tips make up the majority of their income. The act of tipping has become more controversial in recent years with customers who resent having to shell out more and more money to pay the staff. A reasonable tip is now 18 percent or more in an upscale restaurant. Some diners tip based on performance, and others always leave a set percentage regardless of service. Every waiter has had a table that absolutely loves everything and leaves a 12 percent tip. Every waitress has had a table she hardly got to during the evening that left a generous tip. Our waitstaff earn an average of 21 percent at dinner and 18 percent at lunch.

In the past the government recognized that most cash tips were difficult to tax as income. With the increase of credit-card usage, the government is trying to pass laws to make it harder to not claim cash tips. One proposed regulation would be to have waitstaff claim their cash tips at 2 percent lower than their credit-card tips. If they earned 19 percent in credit-card tips, they would have to claim 17 percent of their cash sales as tips. This is obviously being met with some resistance. Waitstaff would like to not pay income taxes on their tips, and cash tips may be well below credit-card tips.

The government's current solution to this tip-claiming problem has been to hold the restaurants responsible. After each shift our waitstaff claim their tips on their time cards and sign their names. When I submit payroll to the processing company, I include their tip claims. If the staff claims too low, I can be held responsible. This happened to the Bubble Room restaurant in Florida. They claimed a cash tip rate of 1.4 percent even though their credit-card tips were 16.4 percent. The government tried to get them to pay taxes on the tips that weren't claimed. The case has gone through so many appeals that I'm not sure if they were ultimately held responsible.

It would probably be easier on restaurants and diners who don't want to deal with tipping to just pay the waitstaff fifteen dollars per hour, but I'm not sure that the customers would want to pay 18 percent more for food and alcohol even if they didn't have to tip. I also don't think most wait-staff would want the flat rate. Good waiters usually like the challenge of earning a tip even if it is inconsistent, and they wouldn't want to give up the chance to make more than fifteen dollars an hour.

The amount of money made in a short dinner shift while waiting on tables gives the waitstaff a flexible schedule that allows them to do the things that are important to them. A waiter can spend the morning with his children, see them off to school, and spend the afternoon with them when they return. A waitress could go skiing. She could travel and always find work. She could become a manager and own her own restaurant someday. Or she could be content with playing tennis in her free time for the rest of her life.

Being a waiter is a respectable position held by people who are capable of multitasking and dealing with the public, skills many of us don't have. It really isn't as easy as just taking an order, putting down plates, and picking them up.

I'm glad that the NRA is struggling to change the public's perception of restaurant work leading to dead-end burger-flipping jobs, but I wish that they would spend more of their resources on educating employers about the proper way to treat their employees. My sister Devin will never work in another restaurant, and it's not just because I fired her for not coming to work. (I had no idea that she was really sick. I thought that she was faking.)

When she was fifteen and illegally employed at her first

restaurant job, she bussed tables in the dining room while I helped with banquet service in the ballroom. She was young, terrified, looked seventeen or nineteen, and was treated accordingly. Devin was having a particularly bad lunch one day after a customer called her stupid because she didn't know what the soup was. Shaken from this encounter, she broke a glass in the kitchen after clearing a table. The dishwashing area was always piled up to the glass racks during banquet service. When Devin broke a second glass less than fifteen minutes later, the owner said, "Tell that bitch to stop breaking my glasses." After she burst into tears, I took her home, and she never went back. She now has a part-time job at a convenience store while she attends college, but she will never go into a restaurant unless she's there to eat.

Devin's not the only one. I recently spoke with a friend who had waitressed and bartended for years while trying to support her two children and complete school. While she was working in a bar fifteen years ago, the owner told all the waitresses they had to sleep with him in order to keep their jobs. She refused, but he was still aggressive. One packed Saturday night, the drunken owner bit her chest and announced that he owned her. The next day she consulted an attorney. He told her she would probably lose her job when she filed the lawsuit. Could she support her family for six months or longer until they won the case—assuming they did win? It was a small town, and she knew she would be blacklisted from the rest of the bars and restaurants. She also didn't think that she could win the case even with all of the witnesses. The three employees working that night wouldn't testify. One, a female, couldn't afford to lose her job, and the two male employees were related to the owner. She thought about her children while she kept on working. The bar is still there, but I don't think it has the same owner.

I also heard about a restaurant in our area being sued for forcing a woman of Indian heritage to wear a dot on her forehead and kiss the dishwasher before she was allowed to go home. The owner of this place is the same guy who Dumpster-dives in the grocery store parking lot for expired muffins and bagels to serve at brunch. Incidents like these make me ashamed to be in this business. I don't understand why these things happen, and I shudder when I wonder about the illegal, unethical, and threatening situations that go unreported each day. The key to survival is to make good decisions. Don't work in places where you aren't comfortable, and don't stay where you aren't treated with respect.

Easier said than done. Most of the time it's the customers who don't treat the waitstaff with respect, not the owners or fellow employees. Customers feel they have a right to insult the clothing you wear because they are buying a meal.

There are so many things that can go wrong. The waitress may have been slow in delivering the food, the kitchen could have been short staffed, the chef could be training someone new. Most chefs strive for excellence in what they do, but not every night can be perfect. The dining public has no idea what it is like for a chef to work fifteen sixteen-hour days in a row. Chris could hardly remember his name after he worked those kind of hours in short-staffed kitchens. Customers sit down after a long, hard eight hours of work and expect everything to be perfect. They treat the waitstaff like their personal rent-a-slaves for the night and expect the chef to wander by during the evening for a casual conversation about why they feel he should add their aunt Margaret's tuna casserole (it's special—she adds graham crackers to the mixture) to his upscale French menu. And you wonder why the chef never wants to leave the kitchen?

Of course, I'm not saying waiters are always right and the customer is always wrong. When you eat out as often as we do, you will have many more bad waiters than good ones. Nothing bothers me more than watching a group of waitstaff gossiping in the service station while you lick the condensation off the side of your glass in panicked desperation waiting for water. I also can't stand the "Hello, my name is Melissa. I'll be your server this evening. Can I start you off with our deep-fried lumps of fat that will cause you to drink twenty-five dollars in beer before your entrée arrives?" There is a chain restaurant in town that takes the hello-my-name-is shtick a little farther. The waitstaff actually write their names upside down in crayon on the paper tablecloth, then pour olive oil on a bread plate. "This is our Italian butter." Um. No, it's not, Melissa. It's olive oil with pepper in it. Melissa, can I just have a club soda, please? Thanks, Melissa. Hey, what's your last name? Can I stalk you?

Another annoying waitstaff habit is the play-by-play of your meal. We have a waiter who does it at Metro Bis on occasion. It's a hard habit to break if you've been doing it for a long time. It always starts when you sit down. The waitress runs by and says, "I'll be with you in just a minute. I just have to drop off these drinks." No big deal. She comes back with her hello-my-name-is spiel and takes a drink order. "I'll be right back with your drinks." Okay. "Here are your drinks. Let's see, we have a club soda and a Bass Ale. Are you ready to order? A salad, a burger medium, and a pasta. I'll bring out your salad, and then I'll bring your burger and pasta." Uh-huh. "Here's your salad. I just got three other tables and I won't be back for a while. Do you need any drinks?" Nope. "Can I clear your salad plate? Do you want another beer? I'm going to get your entrées now." Hmm. "Here are your entrées. Would you like pepper or cheese on that? Let me get you a fork. I forgot your beer. Do you want a club soda?" No pepper, thanks. We didn't order a beer. "Oh, here's your fork. How are your entrées? Ha-ha. You haven't tried them yet because you don't have a fork. Let me know if you need anything else." A hole in the head, maybe? I know that she's just being nice, but maybe

Melissa should just pull up a chair. She's interrupted our conversation so many times that I just want to strangle her when she comes to the table. It also doesn't help that Chris just completely ignores her. I have to respond to each of her questions every ten minutes while trying to eat my meal. I know that she's just being helpful, but I don't have to be told my entrée is coming after my salad. I feel pretty confident that it is on its way.

This type of service is mostly found in family restaurants, where parents like to be reassured that the kitchen has not forgotten their starving children and the food is coming before the kids eat all the crayons. In upscale establishments the waiters have different bad habits. If Chris orders a fifty-dollar bottle of wine for the table, the waiter should be able to open it. He shouldn't have to ask for silverware and he shouldn't have to wonder if the waiter forgot his coffee.

Mistakes happen everywhere, and no restaurant is perfect. I understand why these tasks aren't always completed properly, but I can't understand the language that waiters in upscale restaurants use. At a casual place the waiter stops by and asks, "Is everything okay?" It's much easier to just say yes, even if everything sucks, so that the waiter will go away. In upscale restaurants it is assumed that everything is okay, and the waiter is not supposed to force a response from the diner. The manager will stop by the table and check in, but the waiter is not supposed to ask. But some waiters were trained to ask from their first days in a dining room, and they can't help but say something after the food arrives. The most common question is, "Is everything to your liking?" or "Is everything to your taste?" I can't stand either, but the worst one that I ever heard was, "Has everything exceeded your expectations?" I had to restrain every muscle in my body so I wouldn't say, "My expectations were so low that they were easy to exceed." Or "My expectations are so high that you will never exceed them."

In the past I have responded to waiters who unwittingly asked me questions that they expected no response from. It's almost like "How are you?" when you don't really care. Or the immortal "Have a nice day." I once had a waiter ask me how my dessert was. I couldn't help it. I told him it was icky. You should have seen the look on his face. "What do you mean?" he stammered. At this point I was a little embarrassed by my own response, but I felt there was no turning back. "Well, it's burned on the bottom and not cooked in the middle," I replied. Our dinner companion told the waiter it tasted as if a third-grader were trying to make brownies for the first time. I thought his comment was excessive. It was bad enough when I said the brownie was icky. After the waiter ran to the kitchen and I resisted the urge to crawl under the table, Chris started making fun of me.

"Icky? The dessert is icky? Aren't you an English major? Couldn't you come up with a better word? Icky!"

"There was no better word to describe it," I declared. If the waiter didn't want my opinion of the dessert, he shouldn't have asked.

I try to be on my best behavior when we go out now. I know the business is not easy, and I would rather not contribute to the stress of the waitstaff at any restaurant.

Customers have some annoying habits, too. Unfortunately, they can't be trained. Anyone who has ever waited on a large table is used to the excuse-me-we're-ready-to-order problem. The waiter will carefully examine the table to see if everyone is ready. He might even ask at the far end of the table, just to make sure. "Start with me and they will have decided by the time that you get to them," is usually a clue that the waiter will be trapped at the table for ten to fifteen minutes. The first guy orders, and it turns out that no one else is ready. "What are you having?" "Did you order an appetizer?" "Have you ever had the smoked salmon here?" The waiter tries one last escape: "I can come back." "No, we're ready." Actually you're not, and you are wasting the waiter's time. He has at least five other things that he should be doing.

The only way to annoy him even more would be if someone at that big table (who hasn't ordered yet) gets a cell phone call from the baby-sitter and goes outside to answer it. Cell phones are a touchy subject in restaurants. Some places have statements on their menus telling you not to use your phone, some have stickers on their front doors, and others have designed special rooms for cell phone conversations. It doesn't bother me that much unless someone has a long, stupid song for a ring that they can't hear even though everyone around the table has started to sing along.

There are a few other customer habits that make waiters cringe. Nothing beats that first cold fall day when winter coats are pulled out of their mothball hibernation. The stench of mothballs fills the entire restaurant, and I can't even smell the food in the open kitchen. Then come the holidays, when customers have eaten too much, have gotten larger, and need to spread out into the middle of the path to the kitchen. Some diners push their chairs out as far as they can while still being associated with the table. The waiters race by with a zigzag step similar to those Hawaiian dolls swirling on car dashboards. I can't wait for a worker's comp claim from an employee throwing out his hip while trying to maneuver around the obstruction.

Waiters also try to avoid grabbing hands. One Friday a man clenched Jerry by the arm.

"When will my table be ready?" the guy asked. "Will I be able to eat tonight?"

Jerry yanked his arm away and made it clear he was not to be touched. "I'm setting a table right now, sir."

The man walked out instead of being seated.

Some diners try to yank the plate from the waitress just as she is trying to put it down. The momentum of the food isn't in balance with the plate, and lamb slides perilously back and forth before settling on the table. It's also not a good idea to try to hand a finished plate to the waiter, either, unless the customer is in a very tight spot and the waiter is frantically gesturing for it. A waiter approaches a table with a plan. He will pick up the dinner plates, silverware, bread plates, bread basket, and maybe a few glasses in a certain way. This ensures that he can get everything in one trip. If something is handed to him out of sequence, his gathering procedure is thrown off. Jerry won't take plates for this reason. He'll give a friendly, "I'll get that in a minute," then he'll load up everything on the table and take that dish last, leaving the weary diner to build arm muscles while holding it in midair for forty seconds.

A simple disruption in your plan isn't the worst customer habit. A customer can do nothing more offensive than leave behind his political views and used tissues (ick). Waiters deal with all kinds of people every day. They need to work through their issues of racism and sexism in order to treat every table fairly and equally. During our first six months in business, a customer covered the sink and toilet in the men's and women's rooms with antiabortion stickers. No thanks. Political candidates hound us in the fall to display their posters. If we take a side, we lose half of the customers. What upsets me most is when people try to convert the wait-staff to Christianity by leaving little preprinted religious cards with the tip: "Thank you. I appreciate your service.

Here's a thought to brighten your day—perhaps your whole life! Happiness . . . we long for it; we work for it. But every time we have it, it's gone—like a soap bubble in a child's eager grasp. Happiness is more than our much-too-short two-week vacation or even our 'dream come true.' Real happiness is a quality of life that comes from God alone." And so on. Religion is essential in some people's lives. I understand people wanting to share their faith, but even if we are heathens, we shouldn't be converted with a tip after lunch.

Throughout all interactions with the customer, the wait-staff must convey a competent confidence during the most overwhelming circumstances. While the customer is grumpy that her Bombay on the rocks with a twist hasn't reached the table yet, the dishwasher has run to the package store to buy another bottle because the liquor delivery hasn't arrived and the waitress stops by to reassure the customer that it will just be a couple minutes until she gets that drink. Worse yet, the kitchen is backed up because of a grease spill on the line or a chef has fallen down the back stairway on his way to the walk-in to get more veal chops. "Your dinner will be served shortly," the waitress coos. This is where the diner sets the tone. If she chooses to abuse the waitress when everything doesn't go as planned, her service will probably suffer. Who wants to be treated like crap while doing her job? The more understanding the diner, the better the service will most likely be. After all, the waitress is another human being. The front of the house is the hardest place to work, and the wait-staff are often treated badly. Everything from shouting and snapping to pointing and pinching goes on in the dining room, and service still continues with a smile.

CIVILIANS

*W*ithout the customers there would be no one to wait on. I've always thought it strange to wait on tables and not on people. It would be a lot easier to wait on tables, and a lot more boring, too. There are some people whom we love to see. They are friendly, thoughtful, and considerate. They ask how we are, and they really mean it. There is a couple who comes in at eight o'clock every single Saturday night. They're almost like family. We look forward to the businessman who comes in three times a week. There is a group of Realtors who have lunch once a month. Every Tuesday and Wednesday an advertising agent has lunch on table seven; she created her own salad, which we make just for her. Almost every Saturday lunch there is a couple we love to see whom we call the caviar people. There is a family of four who dine on Fridays—the children eat and enjoy the unaltered entrées off the menu. There are two older couples who come regularly for lunch. Both sit next to each other on the banquette. One couple orders a bowl of soup and splits a sandwich with baby greens instead of pasta salad and talks about their grandchildren. The other couple enjoys two appetizers each, and tells us about what's happening politically in the small town we live in.

There's a couple who comes in for dinner during the week. They always share an order of spring rolls, so we start preparing some as soon as they walk through the door. The wife likes to take my hand in hers and ask me how I stay so thin. They travel quite a bit and bring back menus from everywhere they go. Customers get engaged during dinner, and we arrange the ring on a dessert plate. When one of our waiters had a baby, two different customers gave him gifts. We get Christmas presents, countless olive oils, and lots of advice on how to make the restaurant even better.

There are so many people who make this job worthwhile each day. When we first opened we had a regular customer whom we called Mrs. Bourbon, a friendly woman in her late eighties. She ordered a glass of ice, a ginger ale, and a shot of bourbon with her soup, grilled salmon, and apple tart every day. It was hard for her to see the bill, so we wrote the amount in large numbers for her. Mrs. Bourbon would pull too much money from her purse to pay the bill and the tip, so we would give her back the excess and wish her a good day. Jerry would take her arm and walk her to her car. She would laugh like a little girl and call him Jeffrey. Whenever I saw Mrs. Bourbon in the post office, I would say hello, but she could never remember who I was. As her memory deteriorated, she would show up when we were closed in the afternoon for lunch. Chris would make her salmon anyway while she sat in the empty dining room. Jerry soon realized that Mrs. Bourbon couldn't always remember where she had parked her car or what her car even looked like. He watered down her bourbon in the hope that she would be able to reach her house across the street more safely. She just ended up ordering two. We didn't charge for either one because they were mostly water. One day Mrs. Bourbon stopped coming, and we heard from another customer that she had had a stroke. We really did miss her. She always was so happy and kind. She had great stories that she told over and over again, and she raved about the food every time even though she ate the same meal each day.

Another one of our long-term customers suffers from Lupus. We see her in spurts depending on her health. When she's physically able to leave her house, she always finds me in the building to check on how *I* am doing. I have never met a more thoughtful, generous, and strong person. Sometimes we don't see her for months when the illness immobilizes her, but her husband brings her Chris's Pad Thai and she always calls to thank us.

There are also some customers we find interesting and fun, like the guy who leaves his dog by the back door, the woman who orders the chicken sandwich without the chicken (for nine consecutive lunches), and the woman who used to wait in the parking lot for the staff to get off work hoping to get someone to take her out for a drink. There is a woman who is always cold and allergic to everything under the sun. She has a plastic laminated card that she gives to the kitchen with a list of everything she can't eat. It's a lot of fun to try to come up with something to serve her.

These customers, whom we love to see, have made the restaurant a second home. They feel comfortable being themselves and have let us into their lives in a way that isn't common anymore. This level of comfort can, of course, go a little too far. I fondly remember the couple from an eight-top who disappeared into the bathroom on a busy Saturday night. I didn't even realize they were in there together until I noticed an unusually long line for the women's room. Now, I'm not sure what two people would do in the women's room for twenty minutes, but I have a pretty good idea. Thankfully the men's room is for only one person and the door can be locked. I redirected desperate women to the other facility until the rumpled and giggling couple sprang out of the bathroom.

A friend once suggested that Chris's food was an aphrodisiac after I told her about the woman who came to one of our wine dinners last year. She made the staff pack each of the five courses so she could take the meal home to her husband, who wasn't able to attend the dinner. I carefully saved and wrapped each course, then placed it in a bag for her. At the end of the night when everyone was leaving, I realized she had forgotten the dinner, so I ran out to the parking lot to see if she was still there. I was only ten feet from the car when I realized that the windows were steamy. I also noticed a slight rocking motion. I turned on my heel and raced for the building. I must have looked panicked because Jerry asked me what was wrong while I stood frozen in the entryway with the five-course dinner in a bag.

"I don't think she really wants the meal for her husband," I said.

"Why not? Is she still out there?" he wondered.

"Yeah, she's out there in a steamy, rocking car," I replied.

Jerry and the rest of the waitstaff rushed to the windows.

"Why didn't you knock on the window?"

"I can't see anything."

"Is it the red car?"

"Give me the bag. I'll go knock on the window."

It amazes me that people can feel so comfortable in a restaurant or its parking lot. While I don't want to worry about the bathroom or the cars on a nightly basis, these actions seem to be a strange sort of compliment.

But the customers who really stand out in my mind are the ones who have given us the biggest headaches. I could go on and on and on about miserable people who want to make me more miserable than they are. Diners have enormous expectations when they go out to eat. They want to be pampered, impressed, relaxed, excited, and more. Sometimes expectations are so high that we can never live up to them. We serve good food in a small casual bistro setting, but some people expect upscale menus designed to be enjoyed in a more formal environment. So we have failed to reach their expectations the moment they walk in the door; the rest of the evening is an uphill battle as we attempt to adjust their preconceived notions. We are even affected by expectations out of our control. A customer can have a horrible dining experience because her husband spent the evening talking about their finances and didn't even notice her new dress.

A few weeks ago we ran out of tenderloin on a very busy night. The man on table three was irate. He announced that he was a regular customer (no one had ever seen him before), he had totally lost respect for the establishment, and he would never be coming back. Okay. But he hadn't even ordered yet. The waiter told the kitchen about the situation, and they would have offered the man a petite filet instead, but he was such a jerk that we decided to let him just have his bowl of soup. If this man had said, "Oh no, you're out of tenderloin? I had my heart set on it. It was the reason I made the reservation. I've been here before, and I love the tenderloin. Is there anything else that the kitchen can give me?"—if he'd said this, it would have been completely different.

It seems as though these confrontations always happen on the weekends. Every Friday morning I roll out of bed and wish I could just have Monday back again, which is strange considering how many hours I've worked by the time I get to Friday.

The beginning of the weekend brings in customers who eat out only on the weekend. These are people who are usually celebrating special, once-in-a-lifetime occasions bound to create those infamous unrealistic expectations.

Nothing ever goes perfectly on the weekends and there is always a customer or two who will let me know. Last weekend two separate customers started to leave at the same time. One of them approached Jerry, who looks more in charge than I do. The other customer approached me. My customer was great. He and his wife had just had a wonderful meal and he wanted to know where the wine racks had come from. As I explained their history, I was half listening to the conversation next to me. The woman was very upset and wanted to speak to the owner. She kept on saying that she was from New York. I continued my lengthy explanation of the wine racks and prayed that Jerry wasn't going to give me up. Seeing that I was already occupied with a customer, he went to the kitchen and got Chris. It turns out that the woman was enraged because she felt that her wineglasses were inferior to those on the table next to her. She was from New York, where everyone receives good glasses, and she couldn't understand why she didn't get the same glasses as other customers. At Metro Bis we serve higher-end stemware with the more expensive bottles of wine and our regular glasses with the rest of the list. The table next to her had ordered a two-hundred-dollar bottle of wine and she had ordered a thirty-five-dollar bottle. Both were good wines. When she continued to tell Chris that she was from New York, he finally said, "I am, too. What part are you from?"

Another Saturday a customer took me to task for a Bonny Doon Cardinal Zin poster that hung on our wall. Chris loved the poster because the vineyard owner, Randall Graham, had signed it, "No one expects the Spanish inquisition! Absolve yourself of white Zin." There is also a paragraph in the bottom right corner that reads, "It is a cardinal Zin to be inordinately proud of this wildly spicy, full bodied paean to little red fruit, the envy of those who try, and fail. We anticipate it's greedy acquisition by consumers lusting for a complete gluttonous, sorry, that supersonic gastronomic experience. This wine will complement all manner of game and other wild beasts, including sloth." The rest of the poster has a sinister-looking character dressed as a cardinal with a claw and some horns, but it's totally up to interpretation. This man didn't take it that well and asked me if I had anti-gay, anti-black, and anti-Jewish posters that I could put with my anti-Christian one. I don't think the artist had intended the poster to be offensive, but we removed it.

There are some customers whom we dread. When the waitstaff see their names in the book, they all start trying to suck up to me.

"Please, please, please don't put them in my section."

"He hates me more than he hates you, and I had them last time."

"Courtney, I will totally wash and vacuum your car if you put them on the other side of the dining room."

There aren't too many of these people, but they sure do leave an impression. I've had only one customer whom all the waitstaff refused to serve.

"We're servers, not servants."

"I would rather lose my job than wait on that asshole again."

I can't blame them. Last time this customer came for dinner, he tried to get the waiter to stay at the table the entire night. It was Saturday night. It was busy. He had a million questions about everything. Is there pepper in the beet salad? Can you make the potatoes with no butter? Do you have any broccoli? My wife loves broccoli. Tell the chef that I want my salmon poached, not grilled. My chair isn't very comfortable. Don't you have any pillows? I requested clam chowder last time I was here. How come it isn't on the menu? Did they at least put the cheesecake on like I asked? I don't like this song. Can you reprogram the CD player? Your wine prices are too high. Last time we were here we had a very nice pink wine and it was only three dollars a glass. We are going to need separate checks. The soap in the men's room is more appropriate for the women's room. I don't want to smell like flowers after I go to the bathroom. The paper on the table is getting caught on my jacket buttons. Remove the paper from the table, and the next time I come in, I want my table set with just linen. This is ridiculous. Tell Courtney I want to see her right away.

At the end of the meal, after being rude, belligerent, and snapping his fingers all night long, he paid his bill and got his coat. Then he went back to the table and took back the tip he'd left. Waitstaff aren't thrilled about being treated badly or tipped poorly, but when a customer does both, he earns a special place in their hearts. Our staff pools their tips, so everyone was affected, and this gentleman had called all of the waitstaff to his table during his meal with his litany of complaints.

There is always someone who wants to take an unfinished bottle of wine home. This is a violation of Connecticut liquor laws. Once the alcohol is in the building, it can't leave unless it's inside the customer. We insist they can't take it; they insist they paid for it. After this kind of interaction, I just want to go to the office, crawl under the desk, and die.

There is a couple who comes once a month. The wife hates me, so I'm always thrilled when I see their name in my reservation book. The husband told their waiter last time the only reason they come to the restaurant is for the calamari. I wish they would just order it to go.

It all started on a slow Friday night. I sat them. I talked to them on and off throughout the evening. I ran their food to the table and went back to talk some more and clear the table. I asked her if she was finished. She snarled at me and said she was done. She was unhappy because she didn't like potatoes, potatoes shouldn't be served with crab cakes, the menu didn't say there were potatoes with the crab cakes. I told her the menu did in fact say that Yukon Gold potato mash is served with the crab cakes, but we serve the crab cakes with greens at lunch and we could have easily made a substitution if she had asked. As she continued listing the twenty-five reasons that crab cakes and potatoes should never be served together, my arms started to ache, then burn, as I nearly collapsed under the weight of the entire table's worth of dishes I was holding.

Why had she ordered the crab cakes? Why didn't she tell the waitress she wanted something else instead? Why did she wait until she had finished her meal to let me know she didn't like potatoes? Who did she think she was talking to about the pairing of the crab cakes with the potatoes? "IF YOU DON'T LIKE IT, DON'T ORDER IT," I wanted to scream. At that point I knew I could do nothing to fix the situation, since she had already eaten the crab cakes, and when I felt I couldn't hold the dishes any longer, I left for the kitchen. She glared at me during the rest of the evening and left a snippy little note with her bill.

I'm sure I wasn't an angel and you could probably tell that I was completely annoyed. She wrote that crab cakes shouldn't go with potatoes, that I didn't care, and that she was very embarrassed. They came back less than a month later because the guy likes the damn calamari. He greeted me at the door while she burned a hole through my head with her eyes. I sat them and she glared at me all night long. Since then nothing much has changed.

Holidays are usually worse than weekends because expectations are even higher. I particularly dislike Mother's Day. It seems as if every person in the world wants to take his mother out for the perfect holiday meal. Whenever someone thinks that everything is going to be perfect, it never is.

But the worst part is when I know that their holiday wasn't perfect. When their holiday wasn't even good. When I am embarrassed to even be seen working in the place. My worst Mother's Day ever was in a restaurant that specialized in catering. The owner had decided that we would take as many Mother's Day reservations as the space would allow. He also decided that we would seat people not only in the dining room and the banquet hall but also in the parlor, the two private rooms, and the bar.

After the first three hundred people showed up, I should have just gone home. I was in charge of making sure that the two buffet lines were kept stocked throughout the day. Only two buffet lines. Two. Two for three hundred people who had to be out in time for the next three hundred and the two hundred after that.

When the owner asked Chris's brother Bernie, who was running the banquet kitchen at the Marriott Marquis in

Times Square at that time, how many buffet lines he should have, Bernie said four, and that people should be able to go down both sides of the line. Our first huge mistake was that we had only two and they were one-sided. The second problem: The chef in charge of ordering had a good idea about the amount of food we needed, but the owner disagreed with him. Throughout the week before that fateful day, as the reservations multiplied like rats, the chef began ordering extra food behind the owner's back. Even still, whenever I walked through the kitchen during that week, he would moan, "There's just not enough."

As the first groups of happy diners made their way for the buffet, I realized that it wasn't going to be very easy to maintain the two food lines at the same time. I was soon running from one line to the kitchen to the other line and back to the kitchen. All at once we would be out of four or five items. The kitchen was struggling to keep up. They didn't have enough hotel pans for the chafing dishes. I took back dirty pans, and they just refilled them. It wasn't the most perfect presentation, but it worked.

The highlight of my day came while I was refilling the buffet line in the dining room. I was forced to cut through the line all afternoon, which the customers found rather annoying. Once during my trip through I could hear the owner swearing like an angry rapper at the top of his lungs. The entire buffet line could hear everything that he was saying. As I asked for more eggs Benedict, I told him that the entire dining room could hear him. His response was, "I don't give a flying fuck who can hear me. It's my restaurant, and I'll say whatever the goddamn mother-fucking thing that I want to fucking say. I need more fucking eggs, now."

People started to complain. The wait to get their food was too long. They couldn't seem to get their drinks from the bar. They didn't feel that the quality of the food was up to their expectations.

"What? There's no shrimp?"

"I would have been better off going to the Ponderosa," another woman exclaimed.

Just when we thought that it couldn't get any worse, the second seating arrived. Thank God that the people from the first seating complained so loudly on their way out that some of the people waiting and waiting and waiting for their tables just left, or we would have run out of food.

Eventually the day ended, and Chris stopped by to see how everything had gone. Customers from the catering facility where I was working had left and crowded the door-way at the restaurant where Chris was working. They begged to be seated and recounted their experiences from earlier in the day. Chris had somehow found room for these people and managed to feed them all.

When Chris arrived at the catering facility that night, he spent the next two hours entering the sales for the day into the computer because none of the waitstaff had been trained to do so. Instead, they added all of the tickets by hand, which was supposed to be faster. As he sat on a stool by the screen in the tiny wait station, he noticed that all of the checks were for the same amount. How could that be? When he looked more closely, he realized that no one had been charged for drinks. Not one. The entire 550 people drank for free. The owner decided a couple of days later to send everyone who had made a reservation a gift certificate for dinner for two. About fifteen of them were used.

Not all holidays are that bad, but many come pretty close. I remember hostessing on New Year's Eve one year with a medical condition that I would be having surgery for in three days. I was in pain. I had a hard time standing up. I was on Percocet. I was hostessing with another girl who was sleeping with the owner. She got to leave at eleven P.M. to go to a party while I hosted the last seating alone, drove home, stopping on occasion to vomit, and went to bed ten minutes before the new year.

I can also remember fondly the man who blamed me for ruining his Father's Day when I was working in that Austrian Swiss place. This is strange; I would have thought that family is what makes the holiday special and not the food. I ordered a lamb chop from the kitchen instead of the veal chop he had wanted. They didn't seem that different to me. They were both chops. And who would have thought that it would take twenty minutes to cook a veal chop? Lamb chops cook so much faster. I guess I should have known the difference.

During the time he was waiting, I gave him some potatoes so that he would have something to eat. He snacked off of his wife's plate and insisted on speaking to the manager. His family ate in silence. The manager took the veal chop off of the bill, and the customer demanded the check right after I put down his plate. He thanked me for ruining his Father's Day and left without even eating the veal chop.

I would have felt worse, but he had ruined his own day. If he was happy and loved his wife and children, I should have been able to serve earthworms, and it shouldn't have made a difference.

Valentine's Day is particularly challenging. We seat our tables according to when the reservation was made, which means that, in general, the people who called ahead are the ones who get the better tables. There are no men who make reservations in advance for this particular holiday. The best tables usually go to the women who understand their husbands' shortcomings and make their own reservations. So we have a situation where many men are calling at the last minute and expecting the best tables. I actually moved one couple to three different tables last year before they got up and walked out because they weren't happy. People should just be glad they can spend the holidays together.

In the beginning it was hard for me to give up celebrating holidays. They just aren't the same when working in a restaurant. Chris never understood why it bothered me. Holidays mark the passing of time. Fourth of July, Halloween,

Christmas, and Memorial Day tell me what time of the year it is and what kind of celebration I should be having. When the holidays go by without being acknowledged, I lose track of time. It is quite easy to go from Labor Day to New Year's without even realizing that it has started to snow.

Most holidays also consist of preparation time. People pick out a costume, go shopping, decorate. There is a sense of anticipation, a need to get ready for the big day. There are get-togethers with friends and family. But all of that is lost when working in a restaurant. My staff is always working when everyone else is having fun. In the beginning it is hard. Especially on New Year's. Everyone is kissing and together and having fun. Then one day restaurant workers realize that holidays aren't all that they are supposed to be. They are created by Hallmark, materialism, and capitalism. God bless America.

I still long for the holidays on occasion, and there are several people on my way home who deserve to be thanked for making my holidays truly special. On Christmas Eve there is a neighborhood that lights candles in white bags and lines the streets with them. The candles are still burning when we drive by at 11:30 P.M. after dinner service. I look forward to the drive home that night. It's the only Christmas moment that I have—alone in my car with my husband driving behind me late at night. The other place that leaves me with holiday spirit is a house on a dangerous corner on the way home. This year they left a jack-o'-lantern burning on Halloween. I almost stopped in the middle of the curve to stare at it. I had forgotten about kids, costumes, pumpkins, and candy.

I'm also amused by the fifteen-foot-high snowman that someone built last year, the homemade skating rink in some guy's front yard, and the house with the five-gallon buckets that are filled with water frozen, then flipped over with candles placed underneath. It's neat to see the flame shimmering in the ice. Considering that it is a miracle if I get flowers on Valentine's Day, I'm fascinated by what lengths people go to during the holidays.

I know that it is my responsibility to make sure that your dining experience is as close to perfect as possible every day of the year, but it's not that easy. Most of the time the customer can help herself during her meal. Sometimes people complain just as they are about to leave that their meal was completely ruined because they didn't get enough bread. These people drive me insane. Why didn't they ask for more during the meal?

Most people don't say anything or they send hate mail, though I've gotten only one a year since we've opened. The first one was written on January 1, 1999, after we had been in business for four and a half months. I was so devastated and confused that I faxed it to Kate, hoping she would help me formulate a response. The crazy guy began his letter by discussing the "vetting" of his restaurant files and his incessant searching for a new favorite place to dine in the area. Then he complained about how his coat was handled, the wait for service, and the lack of chopsticks with the spring rolls. Thankfully he had "the pleasure of listening to the palaver at two nearby tables" to help him through the "crummy service." He went on to say that his food was okay but his steak was "transmogrified" from rare to medium and the demi-glaze served with the lamb was "evidently laid on by a medicine dropper." He also felt that our key lime tart was too small and a glass of Pinot Grigio for five dollars was overpriced, suggesting "chintz a/k/a cuisine nouvelle." After several days of intense distress and arguing with Chris (he didn't think the guy deserved a letter), I responded:

> Thank you for your informative letter regarding your experience on New Year's Eve at Metro Bis. We always appreciate any feedback that can help us to improve the quality of our restaurant. With this in mind, we are assessing your many complaints. I'm sorry that we were unable to reach your standards and become your "favorite in the valley." Good luck in your quest.

Some hate mail isn't all bad. Humor is essential in any type of criticism. Take the poem that a stern man handed me on his way out the door last Valentine's Day.

"Give this to the manager," he said in earnest as he thrust the paper torn from the tabletop into my hand.

It was a holiday. I didn't want to read it and freak out in the middle of service. I kept it in my pocket all night long, but I could feel it rubbing against my leg calling to me. Before the end of service, I just couldn't take it anymore. I unfolded the piece in the back of the kitchen, held my breath, and began to read.

To the Manager—

Roses are red,
Violets are blue.
The food is good
And the service too.

But, we were disappointed
On Valentine's Day
To find Metro Bis as
Light as noonday!

A romantic evening it
Was to have been
But wattage won out
Over cupid
What a sin!

Still in all we hope you
Will find
Our comment offered
With you in mind.

Happy Valentine's Day!

It just doesn't get any better than that unless you count the love letters that we receive.

"We certainly had a fabulous dinner last night."

"I'm telling everyone how wonderful your bistro is."

"On Friday evening my wife, son, and three other friends had dinner at Metro for the first time since you have taken over. All of us thoroughly enjoyed every aspect of the meal. The quality of food, outstanding presentation, and creative menu were most noteworthy. Although we did mind our conscience and did not have dessert, we were envious of those who did. They looked extraordinary."

"I just wanted to extend my gratitude for yet another fine evening at your restaurant! My friends and I have been coming to your restaurant for a couple of years and have never had a complaint about the quality of the food, or the excellent service of the waitstaff."

Despite the negative people who leave F's on my mental-health report card, I still love this business. Most nights people stop at the hostess stand and thank me for the best meal of their lives and take a business card for a friend "who just has to try this place." At Christmas a customer made us an ornament and another gave us fudge. Sometimes a table will bring a bottle of wine for the manager to try, tip the kitchen staff, or buy a bottle of champagne for everyone to enjoy. This doesn't happen too often, and it is incredibly generous of people when it does, but the negative moments hurt too much, and the good ones don't stay long enough. That's not to say that I'm going to be a pussy and go cry in a corner. Chances are that I go back to the kitchen, talk about the prick on table three, and ask if the food is ready for eleven yet.

COUNTING THE CASUALTIES

*T*onight the dining room is quieting down while the kitchen is gearing up for one last burst of energy to get everything clean. David is taking a dessert order off of table seven while Brian polishes silverware. Dean is cleaning the cappuccino machine and Jerry is wiping glasses. On the other side of the line, Alex is breaking down the line and Norman is plating the last desserts. Mohammed is taking out the heavy rubber mats so the floor can be swept, then mopped.

I'm just wandering around making a half-assed attempt to keep out of the way. This is the most superstitious time of the day, and no one even realizes it. The kitchen staff will clean the entire kitchen, but they won't take the pasta water off of the stove until we are officially closed. The waitstaff will complete all of their closing duties, but they won't put away the bread station, dump the coffee, or shut off the espresso machine before they flip the sign. It is strongly believed that the completion of any of these tasks will guarantee the dreaded table that will just sit drinking tea until eleven-thirty. If you put away any of these items or talk about getting out early, you will be taken out back and beaten to a bloody pulp. Well, that might be an exaggeration, but you will receive many dirty looks and a couple of comments like, "Now we're screwed" and "Thanks, now we'll be here until twelve."

No one is challenging the restaurant gods tonight as I watch while the dinner items are organized on a sheet pan for transport to the walk-in. I stand in the runway while Alex unloads the steam table filled with demi, potatoes, and batter for the calamari appetizer. Mohammed is finished sweeping under the prep tables and around everyone's feet, so now he's filling the mop bucket to do the floor and the walk-in. In between the dessert orders, Norman has managed to scrub every inch of stainless steel and cover the salad station with plastic wrap. I wait until the stainless-steel counters are scrubbed and dried before I sit with my feet dangling as the mats are heaved back and forth. I used to stay in the dining room resetting tables and doing other side work, but I don't take a cut from the tip pool and the waitstaff don't always appreciate my efforts. Chris is helping the dishwasher with all of the pots and pans, and I'm starting to feel guilty, tired, bored, and embarrassed about not working, so I head out the back door for the office.

It's very quiet in the office at night. There is no one shopping, the pizza place upstairs is closed, and all of the karate lessons in the studio behind the office are finished. I usually sit at the desk, play a CD, and sort through my paperwork one last time. Sometimes there is one last thing that can be done, like paying a few more bills or preparing another deposit. Tonight there's not much to do since all of the "real" businesses have closed hours ago. I can't call the insurance company for a certificate of insurance, order menu covers, or call back the produce company that had a question about one of my payments. I check my e-mail, stamp a couple of letters, and wait for Chris to come downstairs.

Soon he runs down the stairs, still energized from service. As he opens the door, he says, "No one ordered my lobster gelée."

"No one knows what it is," I reply from the other side of the desk.

"I know, but it's really, really good."

"Try it again tomorrow."

"Ryan quit."

"I'll put an ad in tomorrow."

"What are we doing this weekend?"

"I told you five times that we are going to dinner at Lee's. You are the one who booked it."

"Oh yeah, I forgot. What time do we have to be there?"

Just as I'm about to respond, the intercom rings, with a call from the bar upstairs. It's Jerry.

"We're clear. I need seventy-two dollars for credit-card tips."

I grab the money from the drawer, shut off the computer screen, grab my bag, hit the light, lock the door, and head upstairs.

5
CURTAIN CALL

KICKING BACK AND
HAVING A BEER

*T*he end of the night is probably why most people stay in the restaurant business. When Chris and I get upstairs, Jerry is just putting away the sales reports and is separating the tips. I hand him the seventy-two dollars for credit-card tips owed to the waitstaff and he doles out their money. They all punch out, claim their tips, and grab a beer. Some of the most interesting conversations I've ever had have taken place around a service bar late at night. It always starts with a recap of service so we get it out of our systems and don't have nightmares.

"I can't believe that woman on sixteen. I told her that there were three scoops of ice cream served. She wanted four. I told her that I could charge her extra for the extra scoop. She said, 'Don't you know the dessert guy? Can't you get me an extra scoop for free?' 'Yeah, I know the dessert guy, but I'm not getting you anything for free,' I wanted to say. Just pay the dollar-fifty for the extra scoop!"

"You think that's bad. What about the guy on seven?"

"Oh, I know, he was a prick to me, too."

"How about the women on seventeen? Did you see the rocks on their hands? I don't know how they could lift their forks."

"Forget about seventeen. Did you see the chick on four?"

"Oh, yeah."

"She looked like she'd been ridden hard and gone to bed wet."

"Yeah, she did."

"She's probably seen more dick than a urinal at JFK Airport."

"Oh, that's bad. That's really bad."

"She was nasty."

"Where do these people come from?"

I just shake my head and laugh along with them.

The conversation shifts from service and wine to anthropology and current events, to sports and international economics, to David's ability to selectively listen during service, and so on. The only time I get really bored is when they talk about sports or alcohol. The conversation is generally competitive, with everyone trying to yell his point across. I join in the discussion just as loudly as they do and don't think anything of it until I try to have a regular, polite conversation with someone during my day off. I forget that it is rude to interrupt and yell after spending a lot of time at work.

PARTNERS
IN CRIME

here's always something to gossip about in the restaurant business. Everybody loves a good story. That's what powers the soap-opera market. People who work in restaurants don't get to watch as much TV as the rest of the population and are thrilled and excited by the lives of coworkers. You can sense the energy in the kitchen when the most recent installment of someone's screwed-up life has been made public. Staff members huddle in the corners to get the latest dirt, jokes are flung across the line during service, and the kitchen begins to feel like junior high. We've heard some whoppers in our day.

One of my favorites was about the waiter who just disappeared. He was hired, working well, reliable, a great server, and then he was gone. Completely. The manager called his house for three days until he finally got the full story. It seems this particular waiter was living in a halfway house. No problem; as I said earlier, the restaurant business is all about second chances. When the waiter made enough money, he locked himself in his room for twenty-four hours with the heroin he bought. His housemates banged on the door for hours trying to coax him out. When they woke up in the morning, he was gone. And he was never seen again. I hope that someone eventually found him and he recovered.

I'm also not sure what happened to Pat, one of our line cooks. Pat had recently graduated from CIA and moved home to his parents' house when we hired him. He had planned to go to Chicago after graduation with his fiancée, but ultimately she refused to go. She wanted him to move to the South so they could be near her family. He called off the engagement and went home, which happened to be near our restaurant. We later learned that he had bought her a forty-thousand-dollar, three-carat diamond ring, which he had traded in for a brand-new sports car. A few weeks went by and his ex-fiancée called to tell him that she was pregnant. He didn't know what to do. In a situation like this restaurant workers start betting. There were three-to-one odds that he would be going south. He was gone within two weeks, but not before telling us that his future father-in-law had offered him around three-quarters of a million dollars (I'm not sure on the figure because the story has been warped by too much telling) to marry his daughter. (My accountant suggested that I marry her, given our debt-to-income ratio, or he would.) We haven't heard from Pat since he left. I'm not sure if he ever got married—he was somewhat insulted by the proposition. But I'm pretty sure that he's a daddy by now and living somewhere down South so that he can be with his child.

Sometimes it's better if you leave when everyone is gossiping about you in our kitchen. I'm sure there were times when Al wished he could leave. At one point he dated a waitress who worked for us, and they moved in together across the street from our apartment. There was not a day spent in the kitchen without some sly comment about their living situation. In the end, Al ended up sleeping on Jerry's couch, terrified that the waitress might kill him in the middle of the night.

One employee quit because she needed more time for personal reasons. Imagine my surprise when I found her working at another restaurant in the area. It turns out that when she was working for us she had given a blow job to one employee in the parking lot and slept with another. She was too stressed to come to work.

We had a waiter who was also stressed. He had a cocaine habit that made him shake and sweat. He was always asking for the air-conditioning to be turned up in the middle of March. I was surprised that he could make it through a shift without becoming completely dehydrated. He came to work on a Tuesday freaked out because he had been arrested the night before. The police found crack in his car, but he had no idea it was there. It must have been one of his friends' stashes. We found it hard to believe that a drug addict wouldn't know there was a bag of drugs in his car. He disappeared after the lunch shift.

Marcus, one of our line cooks, had trouble, too. I never

really knew that gambling was a serious addiction. Sure, it's hard to stop, but it isn't a physical problem like alcohol or tobacco. Marcus had just come back from living in Europe and was staying with his in-laws in the next town over with his wife and kid. He was working in another restaurant in the area when our *Metro Mail* newsletter arrived at his in-laws'. He liked the menu for our upcoming wine dinner so much that he called to see if we were hiring. We hired him the next day and he eventually quit the first restaurant because they were serving rotten fish and the chef kept on telling him to just squirt some lemon juice over the fetid flesh.

Several months went by. Marcus got kicked out of his in-laws', his marriage ended, and he talked a lot about going back to Europe. To fill his free time and take his mind off of his problems, he decided to get another job. He was fine for a little while—until he started going to the casinos on the coast. We have two of the largest casinos in the world just an hour and a quarter from the restaurant. Marcus would arrive at work rumpled, unshaven, and with his head crammed up his ass, having just come from an all-night gambling spree. He often tried to convince our grill cook Chen to go with him.

"All Asians gamble," Marcus insisted.

Chen just laughed and said, "I put my money in the Dumpster tonight instead of going to the casino."

Al, thinking that he might go, asked Marcus about the women at the casino.

Marcus replied soberly, "I don't drink or look at women when I gamble."

The next day Marcus would show up late for work.

"I lost eight hundred dollars last night," he would say with a distant look in his eyes.

A few weeks later he lost his apartment, and we assumed that he would leave for Europe soon. Instead he got a room at the other restaurant that he was working in. When he came in two hours late one day, Chris pulled him aside.

Marcus just said, "I owe the other guy I'm working for a lot of money. I've been working there for free to pay him back."

He apologized for being late over and over, promised that he would never be late again, and never showed up for work the next day. I haven't seen him since. Marcus called a coworker a few days later and asked him to pick up his check. I had already mailed it to the address he had given me for his in-laws. I figured that his wife and three-year-old would be better off with the money, anyway. I can't imagine the uncontrollable drive that must consume someone to the point that they would drive more than an hour every day in order to gamble. It must be the adrenaline rush that keeps the gambler going. When I was in college near the casinos, a woman jumped to her death from the Thames River bridge. She was in her thirties, had a bunch of kids, and felt overwhelmed by her gambling debt. Sometimes I wonder where Marcus will end up.

It's sad that employees have so many problems, but it's common for restaurateurs to help out whenever they can. In the early days, one of Chris's employers co-signed his car loan, and I've heard of other restaurant owners in the state who have co-signed home loans, allowed staff to sleep in the dining room, and even given waiters a place to live in their homes. I draw the line before signing for loans, but the generosity in the restaurant industry is unbelievable. In just one week this year I got information on how to complete a GED, attended divorce court, and found a homeless employee a place to sleep before putting him on a bus back to Detroit. Jerry always tells me that I do way too much for the employees, but we paid for him to relocate his family to Connecticut when we first started the business. He draws the line at helping employees with money. Jerry would kill me if he knew how often I advance money to the staff.

Restaurant people don't usually have the same life skills that others take for granted. Most spend all of their money as soon as they get it. One buys wine, another follows Phish, one loves CDs or cocaine, but none of them have health insurance, life insurance, or retirement funds. The people who work for us are good people. They are caring, compassionate, energetic, committed, and highly motivated. This is not the kind of job that you can do by yourself. I can't wait tables, plate desserts, do dishes, prepare a catering, balance books, and order wine all at once. Every restaurateur who complains about the labor shortage doesn't treat his employees with respect. Working without the right people is like trying to play foosball by yourself. If employees have personal problems, the job is probably the only thing that keeps them going. I hope that someday I can make enough money to offer our employees the benefits a receptionist working forty hours a week usually enjoys.

Not all my employees have major addictions or life crises. Some people are just making money to pay for school or saving for their next job. They never will need anything but a job from an employer no matter where they go. Our waiter Little Chris is a good example. An undergraduate at the University of Connecticut, he is president of the student body and is the student representative on the university's board of trustees. He plans on going to law school and hopes to become a diplomat. There's not much that we can do for Little Chris that he hasn't already done for himself. Sometimes employees just need to talk about their marriages or their conflicts with one another. They need to be reassured about their jobs. Or they just want a little bit of help with résumés, leases, anniversary gifts, taxes, or health insurance. A couple of phone calls, a little bit of advice, and they are on their way.

Alyssa, one of our waitresses, paced the hallway outside of my office. She glanced in sideways at me while I talked with the building manager about nothing. I figured that she was after some of the napkins that are stored in the office, but she was hesitating because she was worried about interrupting my conversation. I told her it was okay to come in, but she kept on walking by, waiting for my conversation to end. By the time that the manager left, dinner service had begun. Alyssa approached my desk quickly, stopped abruptly, and blurted, "This is going to sound really weird. I'm pregnant."

I paused for a moment. "Is this a good thing or a bad thing?"

"A good thing. I think. I mean, not really good for right now. Would have been better later on, but it's still good."

"Oh, well, that's good, then," I replied. I wasn't too sure why she was telling me this unless she just needed to tell someone.

"I just wanted to let you know," she continued.

I asked when she was due. Not for another eight months.

"Are you planning on working until then?" I inquired. The last two pregnant women who worked for us quit during their fourth month.

"I wasn't sure if you would want me to work on the floor when I'm pregnant. I know that it looks bad, and I wasn't sure what you would want."

"I don't care what you look like," I insisted. "Work upstairs for as long as you can, then go work in Express."

"Oh, okay, thank you so much. I was so worried. I've got a table already, and I need to get back upstairs."

As I watched her walk out of the office, I felt uneasy. We would never tell her that she couldn't work because she's pregnant, and not just because it's illegal. Alyssa's a good waitress, and I'd have her on the floor if she wanted to work while pregnant with triplets. It made me sad that she had to ask if she still had a job because I understood why she was worried. The restaurant business isn't always supportive of women's needs.

Everybody's got a story.

"I'm having a baby."

"I need to take my LSATs next Wednesday."

"I can't come to work because my car got repossessed."

"My wife says I have to get another job because we don't have health insurance."

"I'm only working here for a couple weeks so I can make enough money to go on spring break."

"I'm quitting because I make more money braiding horse tails for shows."

"I only want to work Saturdays because I need four hundred dollars for my new-car payment."

"I'd like to take the summer off this year."

"I'm going to Japan for two weeks to see a band."

Sometimes you just have to laugh.

CLOSING UP SHOP

It's pretty late, and the conversation at the bar has shifted to ex-employees. "Remember Tracey? She was so tall you'd have to stand on a five-gallon bucket to do her doggy-style!"

"Didn't Scott do her?"

"Scott and Tracey? It'd be like a dachshund trying to do a Great Dane!"

"Well, on that note, I think it's time to go home," Chris says.

"Who's working lunch tomorrow?"

"Brian is."

Chris dumps the rest of his wine out in the sink behind the bar, then he heads down the length of the dining room to check on the kitchen one last time. The lights are out, the heat is turned down, the doors are locked, the walk-in is at the right temperature, the water from the dishwasher has been drained, the garbage is empty, and the linen has been put out back. The Fry-O-Lator, grill, and ovens are off. The stove burners under the stockpot have been turned low so the stock can simmer all night long. Chris grabs me a yogurt out of the walk-in for breakfast tomorrow and comes back to the front door.

We all freeze for a second while Chris sets the alarm. The waiters grab their coats and aprons, then pile out the door.

"You going home, or do you want to get a drink?"

"I can't go out. I got in trouble for coming home too late last night."

"You're not going to let your wife tell you what to do, are you?"

"If I want a place to sleep tomorrow, then I better go home today."

"All right, I'll see you tomorrow."

The waiters head off to the lower parking, start their cars, and drive away. It's just me, Jerry, and Chris standing next to our cars.

"Did you want me to put a help-wanted ad in the paper?" I ask Jerry.

"Yeah. Did you finish *Metro Mail* today?"

"No, I didn't get to it. Did you finish the wine dinner menu?"

"No, I was waiting for the wine salesman to call."

"Um, he called back around four today," Chris says. "Didn't you get the message that I wrote on the reservation book?"

"No. What page was it on?"

"I don't remember."

"I'll have a menu done tomorrow," Jerry says as he gets in his car.

After he shuts the door, I tell Chris that he's in trouble.

He jumps in his car to avoid a lecture. I get in mine, and we head out of the driveway. I pass the center of town and turn off onto a residential road. I can see the warm light from behind designer curtains and the glow of a TV set in many of the houses I drive by.

I am oddly fascinated by how other people live. The average person gets up around six A.M. or seven A.M., an unbelievable hour. She works from nine A.M. to five P.M., with an hour off in the middle of the day. Now, here's the part that gets me: She leaves work and does something—goes home, eats dinner, or watches TV? What do people do between the time they get home and go to bed? There must be at least five hours of nonworking time a day. Then there are two full days off in a row every week. What do people do with so much time? If I had that much free time, I would be bored to insanity or learn hieroglyphics. I'm told that most people just go home and watch TV until they go to bed.

It's hard to remember what my parents used to do. They had a couple of meetings and activities during the week, but there must have been much more free time to fill. Actually, dinner used to take a long time. My mother made dinner for the family every night of the week, and we all had to sit down and eat together every day. I hated it. I wanted to be in my bedroom by myself. As my adolescent angst grew, I frequently announced I didn't want to eat with "you people." My mother insisted on my presence and I obliged.

Grumpily. If I had a kid like me, I would have left her to rot in her bedroom. I certainly wasn't pleasant dinner company. I wonder if the houses I pass on the way home have grumpy teenagers like I was. Did they have a good dinner tonight? Did they go out? They must have eaten hours ago.

Maybe they went to the grocery store to buy dinner. I am baffled by the grocery store. There seem to be people who go to the grocery store every single day. There are so many foods in boxes. There is a whole row dedicated to potato chips. There are freezers filled with already-made meals. Cans of salt-preserved foods line the aisles. The most fascinating place in the supermarket is the pet-food section. There is an entire row of dead, processed, freeze-dried, or canned animals that we serve to our pets. How bizarre is that? We keep animals that can't feed themselves anymore, so we process their food like ours and serve it up nightly.

We don't have any pets, plants, or kids, but my mom has a bird and my dad has a dog. He was in for dinner tonight, but I didn't really get a chance to talk to him. I should have called my mother. She likes to go for walks on the bike path behind the building and grab a baby-greens salad from Metro Express. I should have talked to my brother and sister today, too. I just didn't get a chance to call them. I'm thinking about the paperwork that never got filled out by that new employee and the *Metro Mail* newsletter that still needs to be written as I pull into the driveway.

6

H O M E

THE CHEF AT HOME

*C*hris pulls in behind me and gets out of his car. "Did you pay the bread company today? He called looking for a check."

"It's been on the bulletin board since last Tuesday," I say as I unlock the house.

I take for granted that he comes home with me every night. Lots of chefs go out and drink after their shifts. They cheat on their wives with the waitresses, hostesses, and line cooks they work with every day. I had a group of chefs tell me once that it isn't their fault they cheat on their wives. "It's the hospitality industry. They make it too easy to get a room."

"Yeah, you just have to call the front desk and you're in."

"Then you call your wife and tell her you have a party. You need to work really late so you're just going to stay over."

"It's too easy."

Chris doesn't have the time or the energy to have an affair, and he would never hurt me. He follows me into the entryway of our apartment, which is filled with fifteen five-gallon water bottles. The water company keeps on dropping them off. Two five-gallon jugs each month get left on the door step, and I keep on forgetting to put the empty ones out to be picked up at night. Just last week I replaced the outside lightbulb for the first time since we moved in, so I might get around to putting those bottles out soon. If I can get past them on my way into the apartment, I'll find several crates filled with aprons, cookbooks, wine coolers, and plastic containers that should go back to the restaurant. We walk by these items every single day, and I still haven't gotten them to my car (not that they would fit, since my car is overflowing with restaurant crap, too). Next in the entryway are five garbage bags filled with clothing for the Salvation Army. By the time the clothes reach the people who need them, most of them will have gone out of style once and be on their way to being back in style again.

If I make it up the stairs to the living space of the apartment (I don't really want to talk about all of the restaurant equipment in the basement—the landlord will get mad), there I will find the dumping ground for everything that a restaurant couple might pick up during an average day. Pens, bottle openers, countless scraps of paper, magazines, cookbooks, wine, and change that I will never have time to roll cover every square inch of flat space in our living room.

The bedroom is a sea of clothing separated according to filth. A pile of clean stuff sits on the floor by the open dresser begging to be filled. The ominous dry-clean-only pile that will be worn until it smells too much rests in the corner. Non-restaurant clothes cascade off a chair on the other side of the room onto the floor, where enough T-shirts to clothe all of Rhode Island sit waiting to spring into duty during a no-clean-clothes emergency. The bed is clear of debris but never gets made. I just think it is an incredible waste of time to move blankets back and forth each day.

There is a small dining room where a clearly never-used table sits with four empty chairs. I got the set for one hundred dollars to make myself feel that our lives were closer to normal. It mocks me as I head to the kitchen. Hundreds of glasses, many spoons, and an occasional plate line the counter. The stove is filled with a few home-cooking essentials. There is one pot, one half sheet pan, a wooden cutting board, and a plastic colander crammed into the oven. My sister always looks in our fridge when she comes to the apartment because she is fascinated by what she might find in there. She was disappointed last year when the fridge was broken for five months before we got around to telling the landlord. Now there are some wayward pickles, a half gallon of sour milk, and a chunk of rock-hard goat cheese. We bring new meaning to aging.

I've heard it a million times: "It must be wonderful to be married to the chef. Does he cook for you all the time? You're so lucky." I grit my teeth, force a smile, and say, "Oh yeah, it's great." I don't want to ruin the illusion even as I'm seething inside. What I really want to say is, "When was the last time that you spent your entire day off shelling lobsters for a charity function?" or "Does your husband smell like dead fish when he gets home?" or "Nope. He only cooks when he's getting paid."

If I had a buck for all of the envious women who think that being married to a chef would be their ultimate utopia, I'd be a millionaire. Sure, a chef eager to impress in the beginning of a relationship might whip up something romantic, but I guarantee that his sous-chef prepared all of the food before it left the restaurant and all the chef had to do was heat it in a couple of saucepans and throw it in the oven. And that's just in the beginning of the relationship. "I cook all day long, and I don't want to cook at home" will later become his reason for not doing it. If he's ever home.

I don't want him to cook tonight, anyway. I'm way too tired to even think about eating. I make my way to the bathroom to start a load of laundry.

The bathroom is a science experiment. Every three weeks I buy a new daily shower cleaner, but nothing seems to help the half-inch-thick soap scum. I always keep up the toilet and the sink, but that shower is trying to kill me. Chris helps clean the bathroom once or twice every five years by dumping a gallon of bleach in the tub. This usually happens during the dead middle of winter, when I'm forced to open the windows and freeze or die of asphyxiation.

Most of my time at home is spent on my hand-me-down blue couch from my parents. I often survey the crud surrounding me and think about getting up to find a garbage bag. It hardly ever happens. Sometimes I stare at our shoes instead of the TV. Chris has green medical clogs with ventilation that can go through the dishwasher. They look like they have gone through the cheese grater. There is a great gash on his clog that extends from his second toe across the side of his foot. On his left shoe there is an inch-long hole on the top where he dropped a knife into his big toe. It was a clean cut and healed quickly, he assures me. Our sous-chef just told me the other day that I need to order Chris new clogs. It must be time if he noticed.

My shoes aren't much better. I don't have any holes yet, but they smell like vomit. The laces are shredded to threads. All of our socks have holes—mine in the toes, his in the heels. I just haven't had time to stop by a store. We always ask our parents for socks, but they are worn out after four months of wear.

The holes in Chris's socks don't really bother him because he is a phenomenal slob. Last week as we were loading the car to go to a charity function, he set a bottle of olive oil and his coffee on the roof as he opened the door. The oil fell over, he reached for it, knocked the coffee all over himself, caught the oil, and got in the car. Thank God for black chef pants. Disconcerted by his lack of coordination, he managed to spill the remains of the coffee all over the inside of the vehicle (yet another reason never to allow a chef in your car). Well, we couldn't leave the restaurant without coffee. Back inside he went for another cup. As I shook my head in the aromatic passenger seat, I glanced in the back and relaxed when I saw his blue chef coat. The white one would have never survived this day. When Chris returned to the car, I inspected his spotty pants and concluded that he would be dry before we arrived. All he said was, "It's just coffee," and we left.

Chris's definition of clean has caused much conflict in our home. In a professional kitchen something is clean once it has been run through the 180-degree dishwasher. At home it's a different story. Chris defines how clean something is by how dirty it used to be. If he burns soup in the bottom of a pot, the pot is obviously dirty. The pot will be scrubbed until it is clean. When a glass is used to drink orange juice, it is not obviously dirty. It is less dirty than the burnt soup at the bottom of the pot even if fruit flies have evolved through five generations in that glass. Therefore the glass requires less washing than the pot because it isn't as dirty. I often find a pot shining like new while flecks of orange pulp are permanently adhered to the side of a glass. There are varying degrees of cleanliness. A counter where raw chicken has been processed is dirty, and Chris will take great care in cleaning it so that no one's health is in danger. The floor in the living room that is covered with dirt might not be clean, but it doesn't pose a health threat, so it isn't a priority. The walk-in floor is dirty and must be mopped; the car floor is covered with two feet of garbage, but it is clean. The chef clothes that were worn while cleaning salmon are dirty; the chef clothes that were worn during lunch on a half-day are clean enough to be worn again. And cologne in the right amount can fix anything.

I wouldn't have noticed the conflict in our definition of clean if Kate hadn't lived with us for four months. Chris's idiosyncrasies that I didn't even notice became glaringly obvious during our cohabitation. His morning phone calls to the purveyors drove her insane. His habit of walking loudly in the morning as if he had forgotten to use his feet since the night before irritated her. Kate couldn't stand the way he smelled, either.

At night, when Chris gets home, he takes a shower, sits on the couch, downs a glass of wine or beer, and watches television. He can't go right to sleep because his head is still spinning from service, and his body is throbbing.

Ever seen someone stand on their feet for sixteen hours? The first thing to go is the back. Chefs move one hundred-pound stockpots from the walk-in to the stove and back again. They lift fifty-pound bags of flour. They take out millions of pounds of garbage a year and hoist it into the huge iron Dumpster behind the restaurant.

The next thing to go is their legs or their feet, depending on their genetic makeup. Most chefs have intense leg or knee pain that can keep them awake at night even when they are fried from serving dinner to five hundred people. Eventually the feet or legs go completely and the chef can't stand up for more than five hours at a time.

This means the chef had better consider his options. Unlike a professional football player who wrecks his knee and cannot play ball again, a chef does not have a million-dollar contract. He has to think ahead to what he will do when his body can no longer perform like it used to. It's sad to watch someone disintegrate right in front of you for nothing but food.

Sometimes Chris lies in an odd cramped position in the middle of the night, perfectly still, because he's found the one position where nothing hurts. I wonder how much longer he can go on and if we'll be out of debt before his body gives out. I wonder what he will do all day if he doesn't cook. I can't picture him doing anything else, and I'm sure that he can't, either.

The only other career that he would be interested in is farming, but he's not very good at it. Several years ago, before Metro Bis owned us, we kept a garden—nothing big or fancy, just fourteen by twenty feet of stubborn land with rusty chicken wire wrapped around the outside. Each spring it was the same. Chris would begin to pester me about the garden, and eventually I would concede and go to the green-house with him. He would spin the seed rack around and around until I felt sick, all the packages blending together, and I couldn't remember what we were there to buy. Chris always bought too much seed and too many plants that could never thrive in the Connecticut climate unless you provided twenty-four-hour care. We didn't.

Chris would begin the planting process by surveying the land. He used bits of rocks and roots to indicate where each item would go. He replanted the pea fence with the kind of metal mallet used to nail the pegs when laying railroad lines. Then he dug trenches for each plant. I sprinkled the seeds; he covered them over. Once finished, I would stare at the bumpy landscape wondering if the watermelon plant would bother to rise from the ground in a futile attempt to bear its fruit.

During the next two weeks Chris would check that patch of land day and night as he left for work and later when he came home. If the garden needed water, he happily hefted the forty-foot hose from the house. Sometimes I would catch him out there smiling at the loose mud. When the first vegetables burst from the soil, he would gleefully identify each one. And then it would stop. He lost all interest in the garden until the tomatoes ripened. The summer was always a busy time, and I would glance at the overgrown mess as I left for work. In the dark when I got home, I would drag the hose over and water the parched earth. When I had time I would pull weeds from around the tomato bushes. When I was hungry and couldn't remember the last time I had gone to the grocery store, I would hunker down between the beans and the peas, swatting the mosquitoes and stuffing my face.

Chris still took a mild interest in the garden. On occasion he would rub the tomatoes and shake his head. We never planted them early enough, and they would never ripen before the first frost. I didn't mind too much; tomatoes have never been my favorite. Summer would slide into fall, and Chris would pick all of those green tomatoes, leaving them on the counter in the kitchen to turn a pallid orange. He never used them, and I would gradually throw them away as they turned to mush. Instead he would buy vine-ripened tomatoes from New Jersey, "the best place for tomatoes." Chris then spent hours with the neighbor's charcoal grill and every vegetable of the season, trying to convince me that barbecuing wasn't just for carnivores.

We had a lot more time back then. Tonight I just have enough time to put a load in the washing machine so I'll have pants to wear tomorrow. I should take the garbage out, do some dishes, wash the towels, and vacuum everywhere, but I'm just sitting on the couch with Chris watching stupid sitcom reruns.

He sips his wine and says, "I'm sorry we didn't get to go out for dinner tonight."

"That's okay. It was busy," I say.

"I know. I just wish that we could spend more time together."

"I'll see you next year," I joke.

"You always say that. I'm serious. I miss you."

"We just don't have time right now."

"I wish we were closed for lunch."

"We can't close for lunch, and we'd be busy doing something else if we were."

"Maybe we can go out next week."

"Maybe," I tell him, but I doubt it. Sales tax is due, and I'm really stressed about money.

I slide off the couch and onto the floor to work on a jigsaw puzzle. I like to do puzzles at the end of the night. It's reassuring to know that each piece has just one place, one position in the big picture. I like nature scenes because I'm not outside much. It's strange that I spend so much time picking out the perfect nature picture because I hardly ever look at the whole thing. I'm usually focused on a color or a pattern in one specific section. I sit on the floor, hunched over, trying to find the proper order of the pieces until my legs fall asleep and my back refuses to straighten without stinging pain. Sometimes Chris tries to help me because he hates to feel left out. He wants to spend time with me when we aren't at work, but he has no patience for puzzles. He quickly gives up, but not until after he has crammed six or seven pieces together that really aren't supposed to fit.

"This damn puzzle would be so much easier to do if we had a hammer," he grumbles. I smile while he goes back to the comfort of the couch.

When I finish I leave the puzzle out for a couple of days and glance at it while I watch TV or put on my shoes in the morning. Then it gets in the way, so I mush the pieces into a pile and put it back in the box. The puzzle goes into the closet or to Goodwill. I have never done the same puzzle twice, even when I have liked the pictures.

Tomorrow is just another day, another puzzle with new

pieces, and I still won't see the whole picture. I'll walk in the front door of the restaurant and find out that the lunch chef is moving to Florida, the walk-in is broken, and NBC 30 wants Chris to do the Sunday cooking segment. I'll sit hunched at my desk on the phone and on the computer until I am interrupted by lunch service. A customer wants more ketchup, table five needs to be reset, and the staff are talking about whether Jeff smokes pot. The afternoon will bring ad agents, menus that need to be typed, and bills that should have been paid the day before. During dinner the computer in the dining room will crash, Express will need more crab cakes, and I'll make a lasagne. At the end of the night I'll go back to my desk, try to remember what time I made an appointment for next Tuesday, stamp my outgoing mail, and stare off into space.

Chris will come to the office, put his feet on the desk, I'll tell him to put them on the floor, and he'll talk about the day. I'll watch him with curious excitement, like I did that afternoon in the kitchen eight years ago, and wonder what kind of picture our pieces will make.

ACKNOWLEDGMENTS

*I*t would have taken much longer for *Wife of the Chef* to become a book if it had not been for Lee White, Toni Allegra, Don Fry, and Jeanne McManus. Lee has been the grandmother of this book and consistently supportive during the conception, baby shower, and birth. Like any mother, she has been critical (she hates the media chapter) and proud (she loves the ending). She has given me space when I needed to work on my own, but she's always been on the other end of the phone when I've needed an honest opinion. Toni orchestrates the Food Writers Symposium at the Greenbrier, which was an essential experience, but she also is a warm, generous, thoughtful person who unconditionally encouraged me. Don will deny having done anything for this book, but he gave me the confidence to move forward and effortlessly put me in contact with all of the right people during the course of one afternoon. Jeanne provided an invaluable opportunity for national recognition, but she also reassured me with her genuine interest in this project and her sense of humor.

Rebecca Staffel is the best cheerleader a writer could have. She's filled to the brim with "You can do it," "You're awesome," and "Go! Go! Go!" Her spirit and positive attitude make her the perfect agent. Pair her with the technical support of Doe Coover and I've got a great team. Roy Finamore has taken a risk by allowing me to express myself in a way I never imagined. Even though his cautious curiosity and quiet midsentence reflections are nerve-racking, he has a passion and enthusiasm I would have never expected from an editor.

The best way to edit a book before turning it in to the publisher is to have other people do it for you. My aunt Ginny McCarthy and friend Debbie Leonard commented on their favorite passages, asked for clarification, and offered helpful advice. Jerry Callahan checked the story for accuracy, told me I should have been harder on Chris, called me an "awful human being," and laughed the entire way through. Kate Manning performed the heavy-duty editing. I'm not sure whether (or not) she enjoyed it, but (believe me) she (clearly) did a great (f——) job eliminating and rephrasing a lot of the (crappy) text. She was also essential in the stress management required for book writing. I couldn't have survived the process without her.

The following people might not think they had much to do with this book, but they all gave me good advice and support when I needed it most. Thanks to: Sharon Bowers and Jennifer Griffin, for helping me understand the process of publishing; Amanda Hesser and Rick Rodgers, for advice on agents; Tony Bourdain and Barbara Lazaroff, for convincing me to express my opinions without apology; Maria Guarnaschelli and Karen Duffy (aka Duff), for their thoughts on the writing process; Lou and Leslie Ekus, for media training through association; Bill Daley, for providing a weekly writing retreat; and Greg Morago, Deborah Hornblow, and Elizabeth Messina, for encouraging me to move forward with an unconventional subject.

I never would have had the time to write a book if it weren't for my exceptional staff. While I do poke fun at them and expose a bit of their private lives, I really appreciate their contributions and commitment to the restaurant. They make coming to work a fun-filled adventure and motivate me to improve and promote the business every day. We work together to achieve a common goal. It is their thoughts, feelings, and hopes that fill this book as much as my own. I wouldn't have made it to where I am today if not for them.

Of course, *Wife of the Chef* would not exist without the husband of the writer, Chris Prosperi, the chef. We have learned to accept, respect, and value each other's faults and merits with the humor vital to any marriage. "They rise or sink together, dwarfed or godlike, bond or free."